A LIFE ON THE LINE

MY UNEXPECTED CAREER IN THE CANADA BORDER SERVICES AGENCY

BY GRANT PATTERSON

INTRODUCTION

I've put off writing this book for a long time, and for many reasons.

Though I started writing eight years ago now, largely as a means of responding to what I saw in my work at the border, I quickly took refuge in the much safer world of fiction. There, I could tell my stories elliptically, with the ready defense of, "Hey, it's just a story" to save me if anyone objected.

But, as a friend of mine pointed out recently, there's no story more compelling than a true story. Thirteen books later, and I'm finally ready to tell the truth. I suppose there's no time like the present to do so. Border security has rarely been a more pressing issue. And there are few issues in public policy that are less well understood.

I spent seventeen years and two months as an officer of the Canada Border Services Agency. Almost all of this time was spent on the front lines, first at Vancouver International Airport, then, and for the bulk of my career, in Pacific Highway District, on the land border with the United States.

I guess what I'm saying is; I'm entitled to my opinions. And, in my opinion, Canada's borders are not being protected in anything like the manner in which they ought to be. But I won't rant here. The whole purpose of writing this book is to illustrate through anecdote. To show, rather than tell.

This is important, in my view, because precious little is known about what goes on at the border. True, there was a very popular TV show, *Border Security: Canada's Front Line*, which ran for three seasons until the secretive and risk-averse mandarins who run the CBSA pulled the pin on it.

You see, the CBSA executives, like civil servants everywhere, I suppose, prefer to work in the shadows. This allows the average citizen little insight into the mechanics of their frontiers beyond their own personal crossing experience, or the bitter anecdotes of disgruntled friends. The media, apart from the occasional glimmer of decent reporting, seems content to engage in the fashionable modern practice of outrage farming, selecting plausible victims with horror stories of perverted, racist Stormtroopers.

The CBSA response is almost never an outraged defense of its dedicated servants. Instead, silence is the answer. And, these days, that's no answer at all.

I'm not here to pretend everyone who works at the border is a fearless exemplar of integrity. You'll read stories of more than one officer who was anything but. Nor am I going to pretend everyone is working their asses off to earn that civil service pension. I've got some stories of heroic levels of laziness in my kitbag, too. To be honest, there was more than one day that I phoned it in myself.

But there are real heroes working at the border. Brilliant questioners. Experts who can find a load of drugs in the body of a car with the skill of an engineer. Crack shots and tough hombres. Professional law enforcers who could stand in the ranks of any police agency in North America, who'd be damned glad to have them. Those people don't really give a shit if you've got any apples in your car, or how much you spent on groceries. They're just expected to ask. And sometimes, they're just engaging you in conversation to see what else leaks out.

I've been retired for three years now. I did everything I wanted to do as a Border Services Officer. Now, I'm a writer and a teacher.

Do I miss it? I miss some of the people. I'd be lying if I said I didn't sometimes dream about it. Sometimes, I'm right back there, chasing a bad guy, breaking a liar's story, reliving that touchdown moment.

But to be honest, that's not often. Life is about looking forward, not backwards. But I'll do it for the few months it takes to write it all down. If only because it needs to be said. You need to know what happens at your borders. From someone who did the job, not a politician or a career civil servant with an agenda.

I'm indebted to my friends still on the job for their insights and support. To my family, for their support and patience. And to my agent and publisher...wait, I don't have an agent and publisher.

Thanks for nothing, assholes.

Grant Patterson
February 2020

ONE

SEND IN THE DOG

It's dark, and cold. Damned dark. I'm pelting down the narrow drive, headed for the duty free, calling out a foot pursuit between sharp stabs of short breath. I'm old, and out of shape, and it's the last foot pursuit I'll ever run.

I'm scared now. *Sunny, where the fuck are you?* My backup is young, strong, and fast, and he's outpaced me by a good 500 metres now, disappearing down the drive and around the corner onto Beach Road.

The bad guy is seriously bad. I just know it. I don't know his name, or his record. But the moment I stopped his motorcycle and had him take off his helmet, seeing the little teardrop tattoo under his eye…I knew. Cops everywhere know things they can't express in words. But I know he's got a gun. Otherwise, why'd he run? A little bag of dope?

Not this guy. This guy's packing. I seriously expect to hear shots now. One hand on my radio, the other on my Beretta, I call out: "Papa Four in pursuit suspect headed south toward Beach Road! I need a vehicle to cut him off. Caution, suspect may be armed!"

I see blue and red lights as one of our cars cuts across the highway. *Please God don't let them run into an ambush.* Still no word from Sunny. "Sierra Two, what's your twenty? What's your twenty?"

"Hey, Papa?"

I look to my left, and there's Brad. He's an FNG. "What?"

"May I borrow your flashlight?"

"No, you may not borrow my fucking flashlight!" Where do they find these guys?

Finally, we come to the corner. I come around, "piecing the pie," cautious, my gun not out yet, but the holster safeties off, worried about paperwork as much as about getting shot. I see Sunny, looking into the dense woods on the side of the road. Two of our cars are booting up the road, Code Three.

"I think he went into these bushes!"

"I think so too. Office, Papa Four, call Surrey and request K9."

"Copy."

There's a line of us now, flashlights making us perfect targets. The bush is thick and dense, and it's impossible to see who might be waiting inside. I'm painfully aware that, if anything heavy goes down here, management will fry us. We're off the port, and even though they're happy to applaud when it all goes well, if we fuck up…

"Peace Officer come out of there with your hands where we can see them! Do it now!" I scream into the blackness. A cloud of my own CO_2 in the still, cold air is my answer. Silence.

There's a turned-out man purse on our side of the fence, but no gun. No dope, either. There has to be a gun.

"Come out with your hands up, now!" Silence.

In the distance, a dog begins to bark. I remember an old ploy my Mountie dad used to use, and I make a decision. "Come out right now, or we're sending in the dog!"

"Okay, okay, don't send the dog! I'm coming out!" Comes a voice from the dark. We hop the fence and cuff him up, then toss him over the other side. It's not easy. He's big, and I feel my age, every minute of it. I'd have cuffed him after he climbed the fence, but I can't chance him running again.

"Where's the gun?"

"I ain't got no gun."

"Sure. What've you done time for?"

"I just got out. Ten years for robbery." Ah-ha.

While we're marching our man back to the office, our "police dog" is located. She's a sweet-tempered pit bull, left abandoned, and tied to a pole by the Visitor Info Centre. We call the SPCA for her. I hope she found a home.

The real police dogs show up, but they can't find the gun. I know there was a gun. The bad guy claims he ran because his bike wasn't insured, which was total bullshit. He had a gun, for sure. I file a Crown on him, and he gets one day in jail for Obstruct PO.

There had to be a gun. I'm just glad we didn't find out the hard way.

TWO

GROCERY COP

Flip the calendar back about fourteen years. I was thirty, working a dead-end, although not terribly difficult security job at Vancouver Airport, running a shift for YVR Security. I was an "acting supervisor", which, although I knew the job inside and out, was as far as I could go without being ex-RCMP. So, I was training my replacement, an amiable ex-copper, when I got word that Canada Customs wanted me to join.

I'd applied out of curiosity more than anything else. My work enforcing security regulations took me into the Customs Hall often, and I got talking to some of the Superintendents there. They encouraged me to apply. I demurred, thinking of the stories I'd heard of border cops hassling people over groceries. A friend of mine from college had told me horrific tales of sorting through the poop of suspected drug swallowers on bedpan vigils. *No thanks.*

"No, no, really, the job has changed, seriously. It's more law enforcement now. Drugs, guns, that sort of thing." Will and Mark were making me an offer I couldn't refuse.

You, see, I'd nurtured serious aspirations of being a cop. I'd busted my ass getting a Criminology degree from Simon Fraser University, volunteering with New Westminster Police, working shitty security jobs in awful places.

I got real close a couple of times. But I had two big problems in my attempts to follow in my father's footsteps. First of all, I was a white male. This was the beginning of affirmative action in policing, and I was the wrong colour, with the wrong plumbing. That was not my fault.

The second problem was entirely my fault. In my late teens, I'd given Cheech and Chong a bit of a run for their money in the smoking weed department. Polygraph testing meant I couldn't hide that fact, so I spent all of my drug-free twenties living that fact down.

By the time I was thirty, going through the end of my first marriage, I'd pretty much given up hope that I'd ever wear a badge and a gun. But Customs seemed like a safe civil service job, so I put in for it. Little did I know what it would eventually morph into.

The testing was ridiculously easy for someone used to police application processes. The "stress" interview was "Plan your high-school reunion." *Seriously?* There was no physical, no polygraph, and the background check was minimalist. I gave two references. They only called one, apparently satisfied by the fact that he was an ex-CSIS counter-spook.

So, it was that, on the last day of February 2000, I arrived at the Customs Hall for my intake training.

*

There were twelve of us, a diverse bunch. I remember some more clearly than others. Tania was a tall brunette with a ribald sense of humour, and we bonded automatically. Graham was a bespectacled ex-soldier who at first seemed humourless, until you understood how subtle and subversive he actually was.

They were not your typical law enforcement recruits, I supposed. Some were, some weren't. Anyway, it really wasn't your typical law enforcement job, that became clear very quickly.

The airport was a controlled environment. With a false sense of security, behind unarmed guards on the access doors, and relying on the often dubious work of security screeners around the world, we proceeded as if weapons were not a real issue.

We learned to focus on three main things: drugs, high-value commodities, and immigration.

The twelve of us learned the basics of questioning, as travellers surged past us in hordes. We examined tickets, queried names in the computers, checked visas, stamped passports. We learned what "High-risk origin and routing" meant. Vietnam, Amsterdam, Bangkok...these were bad places. Single men, travelling alone: also bad. People who'd paid for their tickets, in cash, at the last moment? Bad, bad, bad. Worse still were people who hadn't even paid for their own tickets. The worst of all were people whose photos didn't match their passports or couldn't pronounce the names of their hometowns. Colin, my first Superintendent, caught a Nigerian imposter on an American passport who claimed to be from "Howston" Texas.

Of all things, we learned to look at people's shoes. We were taught that refugees, who thanks to a curious feature of the *Immigration Act* were incentivized to get past us and make an "inland" claim, often splurged on a nice suit to get on the airplane. But they didn't buy new shoes. When I was set free to roam on my own, I tried out this theory, and damned if it didn't work.

We learned that people will go to the most depraved lengths to smuggle. Drugs in their asses. Money stuffed into kid's diapers. Heroin stuffed into rotten meat. We also learned that people would lie when the truth would set them free, and that those lies were usually only three questions deep. More questions than that, and the lie fell apart.

We learned that the average smuggler was hardly Professor Moriarty. They relied on us to be weighed down by the sheer volume of people we had to deal with, and to give in to the subtle, and sometimes not-so-subtle pressure to "keep the traffic moving." If we really zeroed in on them, they were fucked.

We asked permission to do everything. Perform a seizure of goods, make an arrest, perform a strip search. Because our knowledge of policy came before our knowledge of law, only gradually did it dawn on me that this "mother, may I" system was mostly unnecessary. But it also dawned on me that the Agency did not want us to know this. We needed to be controlled, not to think of ourselves the way the law viewed us, as independent actors.

The Agency, or, to be exact, the Canada Customs and Revenue Agency, as it was then known, looked very different back then from what it would later become. Weapons were not carried. I didn't even have a set of handcuffs for my first year. We looked decidedly unmilitary in our tight, medium blue trousers and light blue shirts, known derisively as "bus driver blues." We so closely resembled porters that, more than once, I was offered ten dollars to cart a passenger's bags out of the hall.

Some older female officers wore skirts and heels and carried regulation-issue purses. We had detention cells, but they were rarely used. Arrestees sat, shamefaced, outside the Superintendent's office, like bad pupils waiting to see the Principal. The solution to any outburst of violent behaviour was the "Customs Dogpile," a helter-skelter, reckless, multilayered pummeling of the offending miscreant.

We knew little of terrorism. It was not on the top of our list of concerns. But that would soon change.

THREE

FLYING COLOURS

I was still learning the ropes at VIA when I had my first real showdown with a Biker.

Bikers were often, if not always, trouble. By "Bikers," I'm talking about members and associates of the Hells Angels Motorcycle Club. All of them were on our radar, and since they loved to chase the sun in Mexico, where they were also believed to have numerous "business" interests, the opportunity for confrontation arose often.

When it comes to Bikers, we quickly learned the deal from the old hands. Bikers are not harmless dudes with beards and leather vests who like to ride Harleys. Regardless of their constant attempts to groom their image with Christmas toy runs, Bikers are dope pushers, pimps, and killers.

The Hells Angels ruled almost all of Canada. In Quebec, a war raged between the Rock Machine, the Angels' only serious rival, and the Death's Head boys. Among others, this war would claim two assassinated prison guards, one a single mother, and an eleven-year old boy.

Fuck your toy runs.

The Angels operate in a three-tiered-strata. At the bottom were the Hangarounds, the joe boys who hoped to become members one day and were given the dirtiest and most menial jobs to prove their worth. Next come the Prospects, the guys who've been nominated for full membership, and are thus allowed to wear "bottom rockers" on their leather vests signifying this fact. Last are the Patch Holders, the full members of the gang, with voting status and authorization to wear the winged death's head and the "top rocker" on their leather vest.

Generally speaking, in confrontations with law enforcement, the Hangarounds and Prospects are the most dangerous to deal with. They have more to prove. Some experienced Patch Holders say very little and are even polite and cooperative. They have nothing to prove, so the theatrics are kept to a minimum. Over time, I remembered who these men were, and sought them out to defuse pointless confrontations.

Much of this tension was unnecessary. Bikers do not smuggle drugs. They get other people to it for them. They know their rights and will not be bullied. Only occasionally do they fuck up, like the Prospect who brought a full membership list with him one time. God help him.

But these standoffs toughened us up. You do not know the meaning of tension until you are face-to-face with a hardened gangster. So it happened to me, one night at VIA.

It was a flight from Mazatlan, or as we called it, "Mattressland." Angels sometimes liked to put on their vests once they picked up their bags from the carousel, as a little "fuck you" to law enforcement.

This guy did. He tried walking through my point position, with his wife and kids, wearing his fucking HAMC colours. "Sir, I need you to stop."

"Why?"

"You need to go inside."

"Why? You let me go?" He had a head that looked like it was chiseled out of granite. A vein was already bulging on his cranium.

"I just referred you. Please step inside the secondary area with your bags."

"Why the fuck should I? Huh? Why the fuck are you harassing me, and my family? Fuck you, I am leaving!"

"I will arrest you, stop right there!"

"Go ahead and arrest me, you punk! Fuck you!"

By now, the confrontation had attracted some additional officers to support me. But not many. I'd already noticed that many of our staff did not have the stomach for dealing with the Bikers and would suddenly discover they had other important things to do when the mean men arrived. But the added numbers were enough to get the Patch Holder into secondary for a search.

But I knew it was my call, and hence, my search. Every question was a challenge, every answer was a shouted threat. And I knew I'd get nothing out of it but a hard time.

Yet it was a test of nerves, and I knew I needed to pass it. I knew that a senior Superintendent and a dog handler were watching me. I was also sure a vein was bulging in my head, too.

When it was finally over, and I could wipe another man's spittle off of my goatee, I expected praise for the way I'd handled myself. But that wasn't what I got.

I got shit on for "letting him get to you." I got the very strong feeling that I'd have been better off pretending I didn't see the Biker colours. But of course, I knew that wouldn't have helped me either, if someone had twigged to it after the fact.

For the first time, I sensed the Agency was set up to play a double game. I resolved to play it safer in future.

FOUR

LEARNING THE ROPES

After only two weeks' training, for some reason the Agency considered me and my colleagues free to go into the world as Customs Inspectors.

Of course, this was contingent on our passing Rigaud. The CCRA College at Rigaud, Quebec, between Ottawa and Montreal, was supposed to be a pre-induction training program. But backlogs in training capacity, and the constant demand of the front line for new officers, meant that some officers went to Rigaud after five years or more in the field. Essentially, it was a charade, with the slight possibility of derailing your career. But the drinking and the sex were reported to be awesome. I was kind of looking forward to it, newly single as I was.

But, like all new hires, we started at the bottom. The bottom was the B4 room.

Form B4 was the frequently abused Customs form on which immigrants described the goods which they were bringing with them, and those which they would import later. To judge from the B4 forms I stamped, most Indian women owned at least 100,000 $ in jewelry. To say the process was abused would be an understatement.

Us newbies worked in the B4 room. There, we reviewed and stamped the B4s of the two major types of immigrants: The Chinese, and the Indian. In the early 20th century, we saw very few skilled immigrants. Liberal immigration policy focused on

"We're the Party that Let Grandma In, Vote for Us!" And so, we stamped and stamped.

Occasionally, we met "Investor Class Immigrants." These were almost always Chinese citizens who had deposited 250,000 $ in the same fund in Quebec, with the promise that they would start a business in Canada, and hire at least eight Canadians.

Never in my career did I ever meet an Investor Class Immigrant who had started a business, nor hired a single Canadian. Clearly, it was all a scam.

Very soon, I learned that there were lots of other scams going on under our noses, scams that were ignored, if not tolerated. The refugee process, for instance, was a target of constant ridicule among officers. Every so often, word spread that Immigration, at that time a separate service, was bringing over a "real" refugee for search. These were "Convention" refugees, recruited from UN camps in real hellholes like Sudan or Iraq, for resettlement in Canada. These people had real horror stories to tell.

That was, perhaps, 5% of the refugee traffic we saw. The remainder were economic migrants who didn't want to wait for a visa, or had their applications refused. Sometimes, they'd come up with hilarious attempts to support their phony claims. One Sri Lankan "refugee" doctored photos to show he was in fear of his life because he was a Communist. In one, his disembodied head floated behind a banner. In another, his friends could barely suppress their laughter as they posed as cops and "beat" him.

We also encountered those who'd played the refugee game and won. They'd gotten their Permanent Residence, and of course, immediately returned to those countries they'd been so afraid to go back to six months before. Hey, presto, things are better!

I got very cynical, very quickly. I began to assume that anyone whose lips were moving was lying. That helped me fit right in.

*

The big rite of passage was, or course, the strip search.

Section 98 of the Customs Act allows for officers to conduct a disrobement search of persons suspected of bringing contraband across the border on their person. Officers present the grounds for their suspicion to a senior officer, who either approves or denies the search. In practice, the search is almost always approved. The poor, soon to be naked, traveller, has one more recourse, that is to appeal to a more senior officer to review the search. In the real world, this only delays the inevitable. There is no mechanism for judicial review prior to the search.

Here's the deal: If we say you're getting naked, you're getting naked.

In later years, I'd marvel when I met officers who'd been on the job for years and had never done a strip. In my first year, I must have done forty. The record was eight in one day.

The rules were simple:

-Dumb enough to bring drugs? You're getting naked.
-There's no negotiation. We don't care if you're shy, or Muslim, or whatever. Drop 'em.
-Boys search boys, girls search girls. If you're a girl on the top and a boy on the bottom, we swap out, halfway through.
-No, we don't enjoy it. Trust us.
-If you wind up in a search room, chances are you put yourself there. Getting stripped is a consequence of life choices you've made, not me.
-Officers must not belittle or joke around with a detainee. Show some fucking respect.

I assisted with my first strip in my first month on the job. The next strip I did, I led. I'll never forget the look on the Finnish backpacker's face as Ben and I pulled on our latex gloves. He looked at me with wide eyes, then put two fingers together and made a probing motion. I quickly shook my head. "No, no!" That reminds me of the last rule:

-No probing! There's not enough money in the world to make me stick my fingers in your ass!

One last tale of airport disrobement. I have so many...

I was assisting with a strip conducted by my fellow rookie Lyle. Lyle was very serious. But I already knew that, if embarrassed, he could turn all kinds of different colours. On this strip, he was about to get very embarrassed indeed.

Usually, airport strips are not like border strips. The false sense of safety about weapons leads us as assisting officers to bury our heads in our notebooks. Pants off: time. Underwear off: time. Cheeks spread: time. But this time, something in Lyle's manner, maybe a clearing of his throat, made me look up.

I looked up to see that our passenger had a raging semi-boner.

For some reason, a very purple Lyle hastily concluded the search. When we got out, I ran into Bruce, one of our intelligence officers. In front of Lyle, I regaled him with the tale.

"Hey, Bruce, I think the last guy we stripped really liked Lyle."

"Oh yeah?"

"Shut up, shut up! Don't tell anybody!"

Sorry Lyle. I just had to tell.

FIVE

THESE BOOTS WERE MADE FOR TRIPPING

I'd just gotten new boots issued to me. They hurt like hell and felt like lead weights on my feet.

So, of course, I was going to have to chase someone in them.

Tania and I were holding the Primary Line between major flights. There always had to be someone there, even if there was nothing on the board, in case somebody drifted out of the Customs Controlled Area. Or, in case what was about to happen, happened.

Tania and I were swapping dirty jokes, and generally paying zero attention, when I saw the guy running straight for us. Like a running back headed for the end zone.

"Refugee!" We both shouted and unassed our booths. He zoomed past us, a Chinese guy in an out-of-season parka. "Canada so cold." I ran after him, struggling to keep up with him in my Olive Oyl boots, as Tania sped up behind him.

I've already told you the story of my last foot chase in the Agency. Well this was my first. Sure, I'd been in tons as a rent-a-cop. Some pretty intense ones, as a matter of fact. I even chased a crazy naked woman once (not for recreational purposes). But the boots were a special complication. I had finally found my speed (I was in good shape, then), and I was almost within grabbing reach when I lost my shit.

VIA arrivals carpet is almost exactly the consistency of concrete. That's what I hit with two palms and one knee.

But I was so fucking pissed, I got right up and kept running. This had happened to me before, falling down a flight of stairs in a pursuit, only to jump up and recover in time to steam roller the guy into the side of a truck.

Contempt of Cop is a powerful force. My quarry made the mistake of looking back, and that's when I jumped him like a lion jumps a gazelle. I pinned him to the ground and went for my cuffs, only to notice I had no skin left on my palms. Luckily Devesh showed up and slapped his irons on the guy.

I went to the medical clinic, with all the skin on two hands and one knee gone. I was off for three days. On my way out I ran into the guy I'd just arrested. Immigration had punted him into Canadian society in record time. What are you gonna do?

On the plus side, I finally broke the boots in.

SIX

MINISTERIAL COMPLAINT

I laugh when people say, "Cops can do whatever they want." Hah hah hah.

Oh, how misguided. All law enforcement personnel live in more or less constant fear of complaints. Sometimes, all you have to do is show up in order to get one. The Agency was no slouch in this regard. In fact, they were very diligent in ensuring that their staff were constantly terrified of doing anything.

Every complaint takes at least two to three months to resolve. Considering the amount of work done on resolving the average complaint, which often consists of one or two e-mails asking the officers involved to respond, this seems a bit much. I always wondered how much of that time was simply dedicated to letting us swing and making us think about getting another complaint.

Most complaints are bullshit. They're generated by people who don't like the fact that we're doing our jobs. "I didn't like his tone." "I felt singled out." "I think he chose me because I was (insert ethnicity)." "I've crossed a hundred times with no trouble." These are common refrains.

Of course, the process is necessary, because some officers are, in fact, assholes. And the rest of us know it. But civil service protections mean that very little can come of most complaints anyway, unless they involve some sort of criminal activity. So, it's still a waste of everyone's time, even if the complaint is valid.

Maybe we can do whatever we want. But it never felt like that to me. The aggravation involved in the investigation process made one want to avoid it whenever possible.

One of the funniest complaints I got was one I received when I got back from a holiday in Mexico. I received the complaint e-mail, then did a double-take when I read the date.

"Colin?" I approached my laconic Superintendent. "This couldn't have been me."

"Oh? Well the description sounded like you. Plus, the yelling and everything…"

"Well I must've been yelling pretty loud for them to hear me, since I was in Cancun."

But towards the end of my first year, I got a complaint that was not very funny at all. It was one that made me twist in the wind for a whole nine months. And to this day, the only thing I am convinced saved my career, was that I was vindicated in the most startling and irrevocable way possible.

*

He was a Saudi, a well-dressed gentleman, somewhat haughty and arrogant, having arrived from Riyadh via Frankfurt. His stated purpose of travel was to visit a friend who was attending flight training school on Vancouver Island. Something about that struck me strange at the time, mostly because I wondered why a Saudi would attend flight training here, if there were so many good schools in Europe, far closer to home.

The examination was thorough and long, although not overly so. The man seemed to have extreme religious views, not atypical for Wahabbist Saudis, but concerning nonetheless. But the only thing I seized off of him, funnily enough, was a copy of the Saudia airline in-flight magazine, as hate propaganda, for a scurrilous caricature of "money grubbing Jews."

After the exam was over, I wrote and submitted a report. I couldn't get the whole flight school angle off my mind. But then, I forgot about it, absorbed as I was in my forthcoming departure for Rigaud. Finally, my career was on its way. Provided I passed Rigaud.

Little did I know that the passenger I'd examined had appealed to the highest levels of the Saudi government. And the Saudi government had complained directly to our Department of Foreign Affairs.

When I got back from Rigaud, a real migraine was waiting for me.

SEVEN

BIG SCORE

Many of the annoying and pesky questions you may be asked at a border are aimed at doing exactly one thing: catching a major drug smuggler with no previous intelligence information to single them out. It's called a "Cold Hit," and something dedicated border officers drool over. Many, no matter how dedicated they are, get nowhere, over the course of decades.

It's hard, because you have a limited amount of information to go on, and a limited amount of time to make a decision. Primitive databases provide little help. Concerns about political correctness and complaints make you second-guess yourself. And, even if you make the referral for examination, maybe somebody inexperienced or lazy gets the exam, so it was a waste of time anyway.

Years later, working at Douglas, on the Canada/US Border, I sent in a Mexican-American family twice in a row for examination. They were nice, prosperous-looking, and perfectly friendly. But their reasons for travel made zero fucking sense.

The first time I sent them in, they'd claimed to be visiting an antique shop in Vancouver. I found it hard to believe that the two teenagers in the back would put up with a four-hour round-trip from Seattle without another stop to sweeten the pot, but that was all he had for me. A lie is, after all, only three questions deep.

That time, they were in and out in twenty minutes. I'm sure

there were questions about why these fine people were in for a search. But nobody asked them.

To my astonishment, a few months later, I met them again. This time, they were going to a Canadian Tire.

Now, I knew Senor was full of shit. Only Canadians go to Canadian Tire. That's why it's called fucking Canadian Tire. I sent him in again, and this time, I marked the referral slip with the code for "call me." The FNG doing the search did call me, after he was done. He promised me he'd done a thorough job. Stupid me, I believed him.

Six months later, I was reading the US Customs monthly seizure report when I saw my suspicions confirmed: The Americans had nailed them coming south with 150,000 $ in the radiator. So, what did they have going north? I gritted my teeth.

But a year-and-a-half in, I scored a cold hit touchdown. One of only two big drug seizures I could claim primary credit for in my career. I was working primary at VIA when a man walked up with a Mexican passport and a relaxed attitude.

He seemed to be on a charm offensive. As he casually rested on my booth, he proclaimed himself an architect and a soccer player. Wasn't I impressed?

I flipped through his passport and saw a trip just a month before into Toronto. Why was that? I was reminded again that he was a soccer player, and an architect.

Now, I had my pen out. Trying to bamboozle an officer with tales of your high status and Great Importance to the Whole World is not a winning strategy, word to the wise.

When he wound up in secondary, they found 2.5 kilos of cocaine strapped to his body. I began to feel like I was finally getting the feel of this job.

EIGHT

OPERATION MIND FUCK

What is now the CBSA Learning Centre at Rigaud, Quebec occupies a combination of an old seminary school and a cluster of new buildings on the main highway between Ottawa and Montreal. Rigaud is a rough, Francophone town, and the College is the only game in town.

You wouldn't know it, though. The College and its people are treated as an irritant to be endured, rather than the primary source of the town's wealth. But it's a lovely place, all the same.

In winter, Rigaud lies under a thick blanket of snow, average temperatures hovering around -20 C. The forests around the town are studded with sugar shacks harvesting the sap from the local maples. In fall, the temperatures are 20 C, and the warmth is accompanied by bright fall colours. You can get used to Rigaud, but at first, if you're from the West Coast, it's a shock.

What's more of a shock, is what happens inside the College. I can't remember if it was as a recruit, or five years later, as an instructor, that I first heard the term "Operation Mind Fuck." But it's the best name I ever heard anyone give the recruit training program.

Traditional law enforcement training tends to follow a military-type model. Break recruits down with screaming and flying spit from psychotic drill instructors. Exhaust them with constant physical exertion, designed to change their definition of "impossible" into "could be done." Drill and focus on uniform and deportment, until the recruit begins to see himself as part of an elite organization, separate from mere mortals. This was what I'd always expected, and I was almost looking forward to.

But I'd been warned that Rigaud, and Operation Mind Fuck, was something very different. I was startled, on my arrival, by the slack and slovenly appearance of so many of my fellow recruits, and even some of the instructors. I immediately regretted the boot polish and brushes taking up valuable space in my suitcase, space that should've been given over to vodka. There was no physical activity, unless you counted cross-country skiing on the weekends, and volleyball on Thursday nights. All of this was strictly voluntary.

The main pursuits at Rigaud were, in this order, drinking, sex, and eating.

Alcohol seemed to be the primary fuel on which Operation Mind Fuck ran. Stuck in a no-account town with shitty TV reception and lots of similar-minded twenty-somethings, the average recruit drank every day. The drinking would begin at 1600, as soon as class let out, usually in student rooms, quickly spilling out into the hallways. After dinner, the Vaudreuil Lounge would open, and then the real debauchery would begin. This would quickly lead to the second main activity, sport sex.

Unlike other law enforcement agencies, in the Agency the sex ratio was roughly 50:50. That meant that, attached or not, recruits away from home, lonely, and fuelled by fat paycheques and nothing to spend it on but booze, would get up to all kinds of coital misdeeds. This trouble usually started in the Vaudreuil Lounge.

I remember two generations of mother/daughter bartenders with amazing cleavage, who served almost as advertising for what the VD Lounge, as the wags of course deemed it, stood for. Many relationships did not survive the temptations of the VD Lounge.

In the mornings, we would gorge on unlimited bacon and eggs in the cafeteria, then waddle to our dry as tinder classes. Most recruits gained weight, with the exception of vegetarians, who lost it. Quebec is not big on vegetables, I learned. Classes would adjourn at noon for lunch. Lunch was followed by a mass dump at 1230, in which all recruits returned to their rooms to shit at exactly the same time.

During the afternoons, we would stare out the windows at the long drive leading down the road to the Metro *super Marché*. For those of us whose booze supplies were running low, we knew that, regardless of the weather, we'd be struggling to the Metro like Scott headed for the Pole. Booze was the fuel of Operation Mind Fuck.

Refrigeration was our main obstacle. In order to get a fridge in your room, you needed to supply a doctor's note attesting to your hypoglycemia. Some recruits showed up with ready-made chits for their beer fridge. I was not yet a daily drinker when I arrived at Rigaud, so I was literally left in the cold. This is why I began drinking red wine. Quebecers do not drink cider, and I detested beer. Beer drinkers without fridges took to hanging bags full of Labatt 50 out of their windows, where the bitter Laurentian winds kept their lagers stupidly cold.

As for me, I developed quite a following as both barkeep and deejay. My room was usually the first stop on the road to the VD Lounge.

As for the sex, I shall not tell, except to say in my defence that I was, unlike some, single, and therefore, blameless.

*

To understand why the recruits called it Operation Mind Fuck, some context is needed. Most of the recruits were already somewhat informed about the operation. This was not typically the case five years later when I returned as an instructor.

What this meant, in practice, was that everybody knew the stilted, tortuous way in which we were taught to deal with people was absolute horseshit. Most of us worked at ports where a sixty-second interaction with the average traveller would be considered excessive. Operation Mind Fuck was training us to ask *everyone* seven mandatory questions. Operation Mind Fuck was training us to find the correct tariff classification for *every* single item subject to taxation. And Operation Mind Fuck wanted us to tour-guide talk our way through *every* baggage exam.

"Okay ma'am, now I'm examining your underwear. Now, I am looking in your enormous bra to see if you've got anything hidden there. Now, I'm unscrewing the caps on your precious bottles of scotch to make sure there's no heroin in there! Aren't I clever?"

Anyone with any fucking field experience very quickly realized that doing things the Rigaud Way would ensure perpetual line-ups half-way to Tokyo.

But we were tested on our adherence to its principles, nonetheless. And that meant it all came down to D-1, and D-2.

Determination points were the two times in Rigaud when you needed to sweat over something other than whether or not you should've worn a condom the night before. These were the testing points, the times when your amicable instructors with their helpful tips would be replaced with perpetually scowling Chiefs looking to send a few recruits back to civvy street with a couple of tick marks in the wrong box.

D-1 tested your skills in the primary booth at a land border. Inevitably, one encountered histrionic actors dumping their shit on you, to which you were always expected to respond robotically with canned phrases such as, "I understand how you feel" and "Nobody likes being asked questions."

But D-1 was easy. Remember your seven questions, and don't tell the traveller to go fuck himself, no matter how obnoxious he may be. Cover that, and you had it made. Oh, there were written tests at the same time. But only Kari worried about those.

Kari was the inevitable class valedictorian, a classic overachieving stress case who perpetually pushed a shopping cart full of policy binders around as if it contained a newborn baby. She was famous for two things: One, her obsessive desire to score 100% on every test she wrote. Two, her infamous stink bombing of a Quebec City boutique she commandeered the toilet of, causing Tania to flee into the street in fear of asphyxiation.

The rest of us got pissed the night before our writtens, like every other night. And almost all of us, save the most hapless Torontonians (for some reason, they had a real recruitment problem) passed with zero effort.

But D-2 loomed. The notorious airport secondary test. Miss the drugs in the suitcase, it was said, and you were banished to ignominy. Lucky, we had two paid trips home, on the taxpayer's dime, to blow off steam. Because D-2 didn't bear thinking about.

Tania and I got into our cups and terrorised the passengers on an Air Canada flight to Vancouver. As I watched my friend upend one Bloody Beer after another, I felt compelled to say something.

"Aren't you worried somebody's going to complain, Tonia? (my pet name for her)" I asked her.

"Ah, fuck it, Gront! (her pet name for me). Tits up, baby!"

Tits up, indeed. But D-2 was still out there. And if there was one thing I knew how to do; it was fold under pressure.

NINE

THE STRIPPERS OF MONTREAL

Most of my war stories involve angry bikers and gun-toting psychos. Junkies with fill-blown AIDS. Drug kingpins and dirty fucking pedos.

But this war story is a story of man versus dick. This is a story of the strippers of Montreal.

Montreal is a Latin city. A Catholic city. A city of pleasures, available for indulgence, which can then be easily forgiven at the price of seven Hail Marys and ten Our Fathers.

But I am a Protestant boy, and I hailed from a city in which naked women are not allowed to gyrate on your crotch for ten dollars a song. So, Montreal was a major fucking eye-opener, let me tell you this.

I had heard the legends of Super Sexe, the giant strip playground on St Catherine's Street. My occasional blue-on-blue girlfriend at VIA had even scored a t-shirt. Chez Paris, an even less restrained full-contact club, was talked about in whispers.

I believe it was my fourth weekend in Rigaud when I decided to ride the schoolbus into Montreal for an officially approved outing. I was horny, and I had a pocketful of cash. This led to the inevitable collision with Diana.

I don't know if that was her real name but let me be upfront right now: My life is ruled by women who bear this name.

My late mother was named Diana. My stepmother is named Diane. Five years later I would meet a Brazilian woman named Diana who would become my wife, and the mother of my children.

(Dr Freud scribbles furiously in notebook.)

I cannot escape Dianas. This name is my destiny.

This Diana was exactly what I was drawn to, on this particular Saturday night, a curvaceous blonde pushing 5'10, gorgeous in every imaginable way. She zeroed in on me like a heat-seeking missile finds a Rolls-Royce turbofan, and from then on, I became an ATM disgorging tens and twenties like it was malfunctioning.

In Quebec, you see, strippers are cheap, by comparison to the rest of the country. Ten bucks a song. So, of course, you go for Pink Floyd and King Crimson. But this cheapness is just a ploy.

For in the hands of Diana, every man walks out of Super Sexe a pauper.

I began to regret coming into the Mecca of Strippers on the Rigaud Magic Schoolbus when Diana began to quiz me. Where was I staying? How long would I be in town for? Was I alone?

It's difficult to dash a naked woman's hopes. But it had to be done. *Au revoir, mon Cherie.*

Yes, of course I know it would have cost me a lot more money to have Diana visit me. Don't burst my bubble.

Towards the end of my time in Rigaud, I rode the Magic Schoolbus into town one more time, with my classmates Mike and Trevor. In Super Sexe, we were treated a spectacle worthy of *Penthouse Forum.*

Quebec is popular with American youth, as it's drinking age is eighteen, as opposed to twenty-one. On this particular night, as opposed to the usual frat boys and jarheads, Mike, Trevor and I were joined in the audience by two-dozen college girls.

They got a bit carried away on the peach coolers and sangria. They incited a duo show, then began to crawl towards the stage with five-dollar bills in their mouths.

Imagine the sound of three erections hitting the bottom of a table at once. Montreal is awesome.

TEN

D-2

There are two ways to leave Rigaud. With a job, and your dignity. Or with neither.

If you pass D-2, you breathe a gigantic sigh of relief, go back to your room, call home, and get ready to drink your face off for the next two nights. You need to be careful, because your graduation is conditional on you not doing anything monumentally stupid, but basically, you're safe. You will enjoy a last fling with your temporary squeeze, sit through a lame ceremony with bagpipes irritating your hangover, swear your oath, receive your certificate, trudge on to the Magic Schoolbus with the other lucky bastards, and ride to the airport.

Swearing to yourself that will never, ever, ever go back.

The other way to leave D-2 goes like this: You are either the first one in your class called up for test results, or the last. If it's a massacre, there'll be a half-dozen or more of you weeping in the halls. Some classes do worse than the first wave on Omaha Beach.

Your classmates will eventually figure out what happened. Because passes come back to class. Failures don't. Failures are escorted by a security guard to their room, where they pack, under observation. In a final, humiliating ritual, you are escorted to the front lobby, where a cab is called to take you to the airport.

In the last few weeks of Rigaud, this scenario haunts the dreams of many recruits, who, up till then, had been treating the course as a never-ending bacchanal. Because that's basically what it is. If you have an IQ of over 100, the written testing is no real challenge. But D-2 is different.

Determination Point 2 is the second make-or-break moment of training, and the last. While D-1, at the three-week mark, tested a recruit's ability to memorize seven mandatory questions and pick off blatantly obvious, over-acting simulation participants, D-2, at the end, is a more subtle snake nest.

Supposedly, D-2 measures a recruit's ability to find narcotics in an airport baggage examination. Of course, it bears little resemblance to the recollections of anyone who'd ever done an airport baggage examination.

That's because what the evaluators, veteran officers of Chief level and above, are looking for, is to see if the recruit can achieve the delicate balance of probity and pleasantry the Agency fetishizes over. Get them to give up the drugs, without being rude or threatening. Basically, they expect expert-level suspect handling from entry-level personnel.

This might not be such a problem, except that the training we were being given about how to talk to people was absolute bullshit.

Somewhere in my closet I still have a pamphlet they gave us, entitled "Communicating in Difficult Situations" or some such bumpf. The accompanying DVDs were a real treat to watch. The supposed golden key to being a big tough law enforcer, while getting zero complaints, went something like this:

Traveller: "I'm gonna rip off your face and shit in your eye sockets."

Officer: "I understand how you feel, nobody likes to be searched."

Traveller: "Understand this: I will kill you and your whole family."

Officer: "Everyone gets upset sometimes. Is there anything I can do to help you cooperate in this process?"

Traveller: "Yes. You can kill yourself."

Officer: "Well, let's talk about that."

And so on. Of course, our ever-patient officer always managed to soothe the savage beast with his magic words. In reality, most of the scenarios we were presented with would've ended with Blue Dogpiles in the real world, and any of us with any experience knew it. But we also knew there was no force and no raised voices in this world.

The obsession with saying exactly the right words left most of us, on the edge of D-2, vibrating bundles of nerves. And it led to a dangerous neglect of other useful skills in an examination. Like finding shit.

This neglect would almost send me home, alone, in a cab.

On the day of testing, I entered the room to find a glum, square-headed Scotsman was my evaluator. I'm not long on charm, but if I had any, it would've been of no use. I heard "Scenario On" with my heart hammering in my ears. The "traveller" was an annoying, neurotic lady, and of course she was carrying more tampons than a Russian princess, so I had to be extra discrete when I took them out of her suitcase.

Jesus, I was getting sidetracked. Too much "I understand how you feel," too little "Where's the dope, bitch?" I began to panic. *I couldn't find it. It had to be there. With all that carrying on, it had to be there.*

But I couldn't find it. I saw Chief McHaggis looking at his watch, and took my cue. "Let me help you re-pack, ma'am."

I knew I'd missed it. And when I walked in to face my firing squad, it was fucking obvious.

But I wasn't the first called. Not even close. And people before me came back. I was somewhere near the middle. Or where they doing something new? Was that just a rumour?

"Grant?"

"Yes? Pardon me?"

"Now Grant," Mr Leigh was the boss. He was also, he'd made it known in past encounters, not a fan. His lispy disapproval chased me down the hallways like a wraith, leading to the moment I'd been fearing for the last two weeks. "You didn't meet the requirements of that scenario."

My mouth went dry. In Agency parlance, "Not Met" meant "Will Be Guarding a Construction Site for Minimum Wage Next Week."

"Am I going home?" I managed to croak. The Scotsman glowered at me, and I was sure if he'd had a vote it was not in my favour.

"Well, I called your Chief. He says you're one of his best officers."

I didn't hear much that was said after that. The Scotsman took a run at me, but I no longer gave a shit. All I knew is that the Agency had decided it needed me. And I was going home on the Magic Schoolbus.

Two days later, I sat, my ass bouncing with every pothole we hit, staring back at the great misshapen bulk of the College, thinking to myself: *You've seen the last of me, assholes.*

How wrong I was.

ELEVEN

J-STEP

I returned from training, into the bosom of more training.

In seventeen years as an officer, I swear to God I spent an easy two years in one kind of course or another. The Agency is in love with the proposition, so it seems, that you can make an anyone an anything if you merely give them the right training.

Over the years, I saw timid men whose nickname was "Kitten" turned into Use-Of-Force instructors. Men who'd never made an arrest coached me on making arrests. Women from Air Cargo trained recruits on impaired driving investigation. People like me, who spent another two years of their career on the phone to IT, became experts on the Canadian Police Information Computer.

Had there been a need for it, I am sure the Agency could've produced Hot Air Balloon Pilots. "Here, my certificate says so."

I entered Use-of-Force training for the first time in spring 2001. Recent legislation had ended the Agency's former practice of waving aloha to wanted criminals and drunk drivers, after said wanted criminals and drunk drivers had wasted a couple of people we could've saved. Thereafter, we started learning how to fight.

Now, I already knew all about fighting. I went to a shitty junior high school, where everybody's big brother had gotten tickets from My Dad the Cop. That's where I learned how to fight. Then, I'd spent ten years in private security taking needles and knives off of psychos with my bare hands.

I'd kind of learned to like fighting. But hey, if they wanted to pay me to learn more of it, I was all ears.

The gig was small in those days, so it was pretty much a one-man show, with assistants. Paul was a short, square, mostly humourless man, who looked like he'd been carved out of pure titanium. He was a cage-fighter in his spare time, and rumour had it he'd busted the jaw of a biker in one of his fights.

I believed it. He talked, I listened.

He was obsessed with technique. In those days, getting it perfect was more important than knocking the shit out of the guy and cuffing him. No, you had to get the technique right.

So, the J-Step came to haunt my dreams. The J-Step was a roundhouse kick, designed to deliver the full force of a steel-toed boot to a human thigh. We practised it, over and over, over and over, and over and over.

I literally woke up doing this kick. Of course, I became the hammer in search of a nail, and by the time I finally got to tune someone up with it, they folded like a cheap porno mag. Mission accomplished.

The techniques would change many times over the years, and the equipment would evolve from feet and hands to 147-grain hollow points.

But for some reason, I never forgot that J-Step. I could do it for you now, if you asked. I am sure my brain would love to erase that file, in favour of something more useful, like how to do my own taxes. But the J-Step stays, with the Straight-Arm-Bar-Takedown, the Mandibular Pressure-Point, and the Tactical Reload.

Shit I no longer need taking up prime real-estate in a decaying brain. But, still a hell of a lot more useful than anything I learned at Rigaud.

TWELVE

YOUR FINGER SO LONG

I hadn't been back long when I was handed "the package."

It was big and imposing. It bore the seal of Foreign Affairs, and the e-mail chain indicated the Minister was taking an interest.

My old pal from Saudi Arabia had taken a diplomatic dump on me. I was expected to answer his exaggerated complaints (Three hours with no water! Threats! Intimidation!) in detail, while also justifying how I'd selected Someone Important Whose Oil We Need for a search.

This was at the same time that a Canadian was languishing in a Saudi jail, being tortured and raped, having been framed for what turned out to be an Al-Qaida bombing.

Canada loves to curry favour. It does not speak over a diplomatic whisper. I was no diplomat, but I knew how important Saudi oil was. More important than me. I was worried for my newly resuscitated career, but I tried to put it out of my mind and hope for the best.

In the meantime, things had started to look up for me. I moved onto a new team.

Teams are what it's all about in the Agency. The Agency hates "Team Concept," as they call it. People whose loyalty are to their immediate supervisor and each other are anathema to an organization that demands loyalty flow in only one direction. But even the most blinkered Agency bosses knew that Team

Concept was the only thing that produced happy workers. So, they steamed and grumbled, and let us have one.

My team was great. The boss was a rotund, bearded Quebecois we all called "Uncle Jacques."

Uncle Jacques was so laid back I was sure a nuclear attack warning would produce little more than a raised eyebrow and a muttered "Merde." But he was the perfect boss for a bunch of people who, by and large, knew exactly what they were doing.

I had Paul, a tall, lanky Metis who made me laugh, and was second only to me in the "Takes No Shit" department. Tamara-Like-a-Camera-Pretty-Like-a-Picture, who was. Everyone fit together well, though not too well. This is also a good thing, for reasons I should explain.

On my last team, we also fit together well. Rather too well, in the physical sense, for myself and one officer I was partnered up with. Tailgate parties on the end of the runway after a long afternoon shift led to camping trips, which led to sleepovers, which led to...well, you know.

Blue-on-Blue Action is a fact of modern law enforcement. This was my first experience of it, but it wouldn't be my last. It's fun, but in an operational environment it's just too damned distracting. Jealousies arise. The male need to protect interferes with solid officer judgement.

The key is a team that fits together so well, and not any better. Sexual ambitions are frustrated, or sublimated, and one's focus stays on the work. As it should. My new team was a fine example. I was learning, hitting my stride, and gaining positive notice.

But that fucking ministerial was hanging over my head. I needed distractions. I got one, one night, when Paul came back from a hospital run with a suspected swallower.

In the early 2000's, swallowers were still the gold standard of drug enforcement. Catching a person willing to ingest deadly substances like heroin and cocaine, then sit through a ten-hour flight with the pellets roiling in their stomach acids, now that was tough.

If we suspected a person was a swallower, we could detain them, then do one of two things: We could prevail upon them to consent to an x-ray, which would settle the issue. Most innocent people chose this route, and after a few hours, the question was settled.

If they didn't consent, we'd have to go before a judge. The judge could authorize what was called a "bedpan vigil," in which we held the suspect for up to thirty days while nature took its course. In the meantime, any shits took place on a high-tech contraption known as a "Drug Loo."

The Drug Loo was a high-tech contraption made in Germany, if I had to guess, which required astronaut training to operate. My only attempts to operate it always ended in disaster, with cold water shooting up the chocolate starfish of harmless passengers. Trial and error, I suppose.

But on this particular night, the Vietnamese man Paul et al suspected of being a smuggler had elected for the x-ray. Unfortunately for him, the technician had missed the last few centimetres of his colon. So, he was subjected to a digital examination to resolve the issue.

Paul described the cinema verité show happening behind the exam curtain, in an exaggerated Viet accent.

"Oh…ohhhhhh…ohhhhh…your finger, so long!"

It was a hit. Poor bastard. Our senses of humour didn't get any more sensitive over time.

But we all worried about complaints. And that one was still

hovering over me. I decided I need a staycation. I booked one for the week of September 10, 2001.

THIRTEEN

YOU'D BETTER HURRY IT UP

I'd never taken a staycation before. And I never would again. Bad things happen on staycations.

Ten-hundred-hours, September 11, 2001, I awoke. My dad was on the phone. I opened the curtains. It was a gorgeous, late summer day. All over the continent, not a cloud in the sky.

Sleepy, I noticed more contrails than usual. "What is it, dad?"

"You'd better turn on your TV. We're at war."

"What?" I turned on my TV, to see the South Tower pancaking in on itself. Followed by the North Tower.

"Screech, screech, screech." I didn't know what the noise was in the background. I would later learn it was the personal alarms of 343 murdered firefighters. Yes, we were at war. I called work.

"You calling anyone in yet?"

"Why?"

"What do you mean, 'why?' Haven't you seen the TV?"

"Well, we haven't heard anything yet." I sighed and massaged my temples. The Canada who'd declared war on Japan before the US was a long dead creature. Now, were fat, happy, and complacent.

"I'll call you back." I hopped in the shower, thinking that I knew something about all this but not realizing what, exactly. When I got out the phone was ringing.

"Yes?"

"You'd better come in, they want everyone!"

Complacency to Panic. I call it the "Canadian Two-Step."

"I'm on my way." I drove down the shoulder towards the main terminal, badge held out the window, past the never-ending lines of limos, taxis, minivans. I don't remember where I parked. I ran into the terminal and passed ashen-faced workers, sobbing passengers. On the monitors, UA175 smashed into the South Tower on an endless loop. "Turn that shit off." I admonished one restaurant worker. He looked at my uniform and took the hint.

Clearly, today would not be any ordinary day.

We assembled in secondary, teams of security screeners, Agency officers, Mounties. The intelligence officers' briefing was curt, and slight on detail. "Three hijacked aircraft have hit the WTC and the Pentagon. A fourth, possibly hijacked, has been shot down. There may be as many as three others airborne. US airspace is closed as of ten-thirty. All US-bound flights are being diverted here."

"That's why there's forty jumbos on the tarmac?"

"Yes."

"What's the plan?"

"Every single passenger is searched and processed on Arrivals level. No bags are being released. Aeroguard wands them, we frisk and question them, and the Mounties stand by in case anyone is armed. Questions?"

I suddenly realized what the connection to my ministerial was. I thought of the Saudis. "Saudis, right? How many more?"

"Unknown."

As we filed up to the Arrivals level, my mind was racing. How many teams did they have out there? Was it Bin Laden, or the Iranians? Where was Bush? I saw teams of land border officers being briefed.

"What are they doing here?" I asked a female officer.

"Land border's closed."

"What? They've never done that!"

"Nobody's ever done that, either." She pointed to a monitor. UA175 repeated its death dive.

"Why don't they turn that shit off?"

So began fourteen hours of working in a trance. In years to come, when people would reminisce about where they were on 9/11, I'd think to myself, "I missed it all." Later on, I'd feel lucky.

I had something to do. A part to play, however minor. Mind-numbing work, in the greenhouse terminal, sweat pouring down my face.

Vignettes:

Passengers coming off flights where the Captains had turned off the in-flight entertainment systems to prevent panic. Residents of New York and Washington, DC, seeing UA175 slam into steel and glass, over and over. The tears, the collapses. I felt the hate begin to build.

Four men with Arab faces and uncomprehending looks, roughly handled by us. By then, we knew box-cutter knives and pepper spray was the MO. They didn't have any, but still they disappeared into the custody of the Mounties. I don't know what happened to them.

Patting down a passenger in late afternoon sun. A voice in my ear. "You'd better hurry it up. Hijacked plane, headed right for us." I looked up, and saw a 747, on a suicide course, or so it seemed, an F-15 Eagle on either wing.

I blinked through sweat, too tired to run, too aware of how little good it would do me. "Okay." I said. Suddenly, the Air China 747 set down gently on the runway, the F-15s arcing away on full afterburner, the screaming sound filling my ears.

"Stupid assholes." The Transport Canada Inspector who'd warned me spat. "None of them speak enough fucking English to fly in this airspace."

I nodded numbly and went back to work. After fourteen hours, I drove home. Then I slept for twelve more.

When I woke up the next day, there were no more contrails.

FOURTEEN
ABOUT THAT REPORT

In retrospect, it's pretty clear that, for all the people involved in intelligence gathering and analysis in North America in the months and years leading up to September 11, only three or four people seem to have developed an inkling of what was about to happen.

Let's be precise: I don't claim to have been one of them. But a couple of days after the attack, it seemed like I might have been. I was called in for an interview with one of our intelligence officers.

My Saudi friend, and his pal in flight school, had suddenly aroused an interest in more than whether or not I'd met service standards. According to Al from intelligence, the security services had descended on a flight school on Vancouver Island, and were in the process of interviewing over 400 students. Did I have anything to add to my report?

"Uh, does this mean that complaint is shitcanned?"

"Pretty much."

Sure enough, two weeks later, I got a terse letter explaining the complaint had been found "unsubstantiated." My bosses were at great pains to explain that they'd been in my corner all along.

Sure. I knew my reprieve was a historical accident. I switched into "easy" mode.

Here's the secret about law enforcement work: It's largely self-directed. It can be as easy, or as hard, as you want it to be. If you decide, "Fuck it, bare minimum," then you can do exactly that, and your pay cheque will look exactly the same as the guy who gives it his all.

At the airport, this work ethically-impaired ideal was best achieved on rover rotations.

Rovers backstop the work of the harried primary line officers by "roving" the baggage carousels to find people who need to be examined, and otherwise won't be.

Dedicated rovers engage in detailed conversations with people coming back from high-risk locations like Thailand or the Netherlands, and select exams based on the answers they get. That was me, until I got my ass handed to me on a complaint. Switch to "easy" mode.

Easy mode meant spending the whole morning with your partner on an extended coffee break, until noon approached. Noon heralded the arrival of the first Asian flights. We'd head down to the Customs Hall as the smell of kimchi announced the arrival of Korean Airlines from Inchon.

Easy mode meant going up to the carousel, selecting the person with seven gigantic bags piled on his luggage cart, and "Zero" declared on his declaration card, and saying "Come with me."

It might seem like racial profiling, I guess. But in my mind, it was no different from what I did in later years at the border, waiting for pickups from Nevada and Tennessee, driven by white guys, with gun racks and NRA stickers. You fish at the wet holes, not the dry ones, right?

As the undeclared cigarettes and rice wine spilled onto the exam table, you knew you had your stat for the day. Yes, it was an exercise in cynicism. No, I wasn't protecting Canada from anything besides excessively loud karaoke and second-hand smoke. But what did it matter?

I was fucking bored. I needed a change. So, I put in for a transfer.

FIFTEEN

ANTHRAX

The days after 9/11 were peppered with intermittent security scares, the most memorable of which was the Anthrax Scare of October.

As so often happened in the Agency over the years, complacency was replaced by vibrating tension, bordering on panic. Daily intelligence briefings had us poised to rip the shit out of anyone who "fit the profile."

Needless to say, it was a bad time to be a Muslim.

In October, a series of letters containing Anthrax spores arrived at various locations in the US. Suddenly, bioterror was a reality. Shortly after this, I was on duty when my friends Paul and Bax roved a Pakistani man with a rough story and some very interesting photos showing a fondness for camo wear and posing with AK-47s.

Things got worse when they found a paper envelope in his suitcase containing a white, talc-like substance. Written inside the fold of the envelope in a rough English scrawl was one word: ANTHRAX.

Within 45 minutes, the Customs Hall was deserted. All flights were held or diverted. Staff, save a skeleton crew, were withdrawn. Paul and Bax had been put into an isolation cell next to the Pakistani, with gloves and masks tossed in after them.

A group of us put on masks and gloves and went out to clear the hall of passengers. I stood at point, collecting cards, trying to pretend nothing was happening.

"Uh, is something going on?"

(Muffled voice) "No, no, perfectly normal."

I volunteered to work the skeleton crew on the primary line. Turns out, the skeleton crew was me.

I walked past abandoned suitcases and still-rolling baggage carts, clad in respirator, gown, and gloves. The silence was eerie. In my mind, I replayed every end-of-the-world movie I'd ever seen.

There I was. The Omega Man.

I settled into a primary booth. After about 30 minutes, I heard voices. I got on the radio. "I'm hearing voices. I thought the hall was closed."

"It is." The Superintendent on the other end replied. "Tell them they're not supposed to be here."

I looked at a confused aircrew, shepherding even more confused passengers from US Arrivals. "Uh, well, they're here." I waved the group up. They stared at my Andromeda Strain Halloween Costume. "Come on up."

The Chief Steward was alarmed but composed. "Are we...is everything okay?"

"Officially, yes. Unofficially, no. But here you are."

"But nobody told us anything." She stammered.

"Sounds about right. Listen." I confided in her. "I bet it's a hoax. But we're just playing it safe. We'll keep all your cards, and follow up if we need to."

"Is it Anthrax?"

My eye twitched. "I can't say."

The Superintendent came up, also dressed in Biosafety Chic, and together we processed the trembling people with bland assurances of business as usual. Almost twenty years later, the lesson sticks with me.

If the Government Men tell you everything is cool, it probably isn't. Run for your lives.

It was a hoax, after all. And there were no terrorists on Vancouver Island, either.

SIXTEEN

BORDER RAT

In the spring of 2002, I became a border rat.

The border is different, we were always told. First off, gone were the bus driver blues. I was issued a brand-new, midnight blue uniform, a set of body armour, a couple of cans of OC Spray (pepper spray), an extra set of handcuffs, and an expandable baton.

Whoa. I suddenly felt like a badass, which was fucking ridiculous. I would soon learn that showing up at the border with a can of liquid karate and a less-than-Ron-Jeremy-sized whacky stick was like arriving at the Battle of Hastings with a spork.

But it was quite a change from the airport.

The "border" I refer to, is, of course, the Canada/US land border, at 49 degrees latitude, the straight as an arrow dividing line which proves that cartographers can be as lazy as anyone else. For almost all of its length, the only security features are US Border Patrol cameras and sensors, and the occasional passing BP truck or roaming Mountie.

Though we are "Border Services," and by law have the power to operate anywhere along the 9000-kilometre-long frontier, in theory, we stay confined to the ports-of-entry (POEs). In practice, we get into all kinds of shit off the POEs. Management hates it, except when we make them look good, then it's okay.

Rules? It's a frontier, dude.

POEs dot the 49th parallel at something like 120 different places. Some are seasonal, open only during the summer to accommodate hunting, fishing, and camping. Others are tiny, staffed at times by as few as two officers (that used to be one, but then an officer died alone in suspicious circumstances). Other POEs are massive, like the Windsor, ON crossings, with hundreds of officers. There's also a whole separate frontier with Alaska, which is a crazy place, staffed by people best described as "interesting."

Technically, the RCMP is responsible for doing the job the Border Patrol does on the US side. I say "technically," because in practice very little border patrolling is done on the Canadian side, besides bored CBSA officers looking out their windows and saying "Hey, where's that backpacker going" on the radio.

This is not really the Mounties' fault, at least at an individual level. The RCMP is the greedy octopus of Canadian policing, programmed to grab any policing task not already spoken for, regardless of their intent to actually do the job. The CBSA bosses do not like dealing with the frontier between the ports, because bad people operate there, and when officers encounter bad people, a gun may go off, and someone may lose their cabin in the Laurentians.

This does not stop gung-ho young border rats like me from chasing bad guys all over the place. More on that later.

The border attracts a fundamentally different clientele from the airport. Going to an airport is a big deal for most people. They put on pants. They bring a passport. They know where they are going. They expect a bit of scrutiny. If they arrive at the airport in, say, Seoul with an AK-47 or buck-assed naked, someone is likely to notice and say, "Er, come with me, sir."

None of this applies at the border. For one thing, the border has a regular clientele, people on both sides who feel that, since they cross on a regular basis, they have the God-given right to sail through with no questions asked and no hindrances. These people are now called "NEXUS members." But they have always been there. Probably the worst are the inhabitants of Point Roberts, a little tongue of US territory left there by the lazy cartographers. It is not possible to reach this part of the US without going through Canada.

When Point Roberts people are stopped and questioned, it is like this is the first time anyone has pointed this out to them. "Who the fuck put a border here while I was sleeping?"

Driving, or walking, or riding a bike to the border requires zero planning or consideration. You can be naked, high as fuck, armed to the teeth, or just plain lost. This is what makes the border fun. Law enforcement is work is really only interesting when one deals with a lower class of people.

Trust me, the border has a lower class of people.

But it also has a special grade of mind-numbing tedium, brought to you by the shoppers. Canadians do not, whenever possible, like to spend money in their own country. Though we enjoy slagging off the Americans at every opportunity, we much prefer to buy their stuff. Usually because it is cheaper. Even when it isn't. Gas, groceries, booze, clothes, tires, even the whole fucking car, Canadians want American stuff, and believe the nosy man in the booth should make chop-chop and let them get it.

When I arrived at the border, I quickly realized I had a lot to learn.

SEVENTEEN

BAD BOYS

It wasn't long after my arrival at the Pacific Highway District that I became tagged as a Bad Boy.

Bad Boys, also known as "Border Cowboys," are a specially despised breed within the upper echelons of the CBSA. They are also known as "people who do their jobs and don't put up with horseshit."

The CBSA, it should be explained, is not fond of such individuals, as it does not really wish to be seen as a law enforcement organization. At the time I transferred to the border, the pace of change was overwhelming the people in charge. Three years before, they'd been expected to do little but move traffic and collect taxes.

Now, with new legislation mandating we arrest criminals for actually committing actual crimes, the bosses were afraid that we might start considering ourselves "the police," which was, in fact, what we were becoming. Windows were getting smashed in. People were getting pepper sprayed. Cells were overflowing.

And so, the disapproving, beady eyes of the management cadre fell upon those taking their new duties the most seriously. These were the Bad Boys. I immediately fell into their ranks, but I was not alone. I arrested someone on my first day. Oops. I didn't know that was a bad thing. I figured the cuffs were issued so I could use them.

The Pacific Highway District was rife with Bad Boys, as it turned out, which was one thing which made it so much fun to work at. This was, in some ways, a historical accident. At this time, police agencies were not hiring many people. But there were a great many seeking such work, so CBSA wound up taking on some of the overflow.

In my opinion then, and nothing has ever happened since to change my mind, the officers I worked with at the border in the years between 2002 and 2009 were the equal or better of any law enforcement officers, anywhere in North America. They challenged me, taught me, and I knew I could count on them to have my back, no matter what.

When their age had passed, and a newer generation had come along to replace them, I would feel the loss. They built a new expectation of what a CBSA officer ought to be. And many of them were Bad Boys, perpetually in shit for one thing or another. Their reward for fearlessly taking on drunks, psychos, and gangbangers was riding the pine in the Admin Superintendent's office, getting one admonishment after another on their files.

Here's a few who stand out in my memory:

Andy was a soldier, a cheerful sort with a talent for winding up in the shit like no other. He would arrest as many people as he could, for whatever he could find, and he really wasn't afraid of anything that came next. It was not unusual to find Andy alone with five dudes, prop-frisked, making a leap over the counter with a swinging baton necessary. One time, I bumped into him with a handcuffed suspect on either hand, and he casually asked, "Hey, Patterson, can you go arrest those two guys over there? I got my hands full here." He was later shamefully used by the CBSA. But he had the last laugh. More on that, later.

Cory was an old-timer who started young, a big man with sidewalls and an imposing walk. It took me about five years there before he'd stop calling me "rookie." By the time I got there, I figured he was lazy, but in retrospect I think he'd just peaked sooner than the rest of us. He had many enemies among the management class, and that made it all the more remarkable when they made him a Superintendent. Possibly to shut him up.

Lyle, he of the strip-search debacle in Chapter 5, was one of the exodus of Bad Boys who'd preceded or followed me to the border. He'd started there as a student, and the border was his natural home. Lyle was nicknamed "Caillou" for his unfortunate resemblance to the whiny cartoon toddler. But there, the similarity ended. Lyle was a no-nonsense law-enforcer of the old-school, a man whose word was enforced without prevarication. He would do anything to bring his man down, smashing windows, spraying OC, chasing, swinging fists, whatever. The thing was, no matter how much management didn't like it, Lyle was smart enough to always have the law on his side.

James was part of the dreaded Team Two. We hated overlapping with Team Two, because they enforced everything, all the time, no matter the time of night or the fucking weather. James was a hulking man whose entire being showed a relentless dedication to the job, and a pit bull's determination to retain his grip on anything once he had bitten it. Working a nightshift with James could be a real pain. But I will say this: There is no person on this earth who I would less like to play hide and seek with. He would never quit. Never. It's perhaps no coincidence that I got my best seizure ever with him. James once famously went toe-to-toe with a Vancouver Fire Department Lieutenant who showed up, berserk and uncooperative at the border. The Lieutenant lost, badly, then whined to the media. The Chief called him and his lawyer up to look at the CCTV footage, at which time all talk of criminal charges disappeared. They still made him sweat a lawsuit for seven years before the clock ran out.

Dal was another part of the airport exodus, and self-assured, one might almost say "cocky" army guy whose knowledge of rules and regulations frustrated the shit out of bosses. I didn't overlap with him much or work with him, until much later. More about him later, in "Shots Fired."

Christian came to the border in my wake, and he was quickly engulfed in the waters of Criminal Code enforcement, as was I. Another guy I didn't overlap with much, our paths crossed for more personal reasons. The guy was relentless, always available to back you up, and the CBSA made him pay for it. Then they made him a manager. See Cory.

Carolyn was proof positive that you did not need to be a "Boy" to be a "Bad Boy." She was almost heart-breakingly beautiful, with a dancer's body, and from appearances only you'd read her for a porcelain doll. Yet if you challenged her, she would fuck you up. Smashed in windows, smashed in heads, she was proof positive that testicles need not be literal. Later on, she married another Bad Boy from US Immigration and Customs Enforcement. If their kids get into law enforcement, you'd best do what they say.

One day, the bosses assembled all the Bad Boys for "diversity" training. They'd detected some non-program thinking in our attitudes, and they brought in an "expert" to re-educate us. I remember looking around and understanding immediately why I was there. Bad Boys, every last one of us.

A couple of hours later, the expert left, promising never to return. We'd taken turns spanking him, rhetorically of course, on his new-age PC bullshit. Look, you can fuck with Bad Boys, but if you're going to tell them they're wrong, you'd better bring more than catchphrases.

EIGHTEEN

TEAM FIVE

I had the very good luck to be absorbed by the most comfortable team imaginable at the border. I have worked on many teams in my career, but this was the only one I truly considered a family.

It was a dysfunctional family, but a family, nonetheless. My transition to the strange new world of the border was made easier by it. That is not to say that I loved working with them all. The cast of characters, added to and subtracted from occasionally by students and fleeting visitors, stayed remarkably stable for four years.

Tina was the Superintendent, a tiny Irish woman with a penchant for chain smoking, who was perpetually enveloped in clouds of perfume. She had a passion for seizing jewelry, something I sadly never met her expectations in, but in most other respects we got along. This was all the more remarkable because she associated with some female superintendents who ate male officers of my kind for breakfast. I was lucky to have her in my corner.

Jack was a former small-town Alberta cop with googly eyes and a talent for lurid stories of banging dispatchers over the photocopier in his old job. He also liked throwing knives around the office, but he was dangerously bad at that. It tended to discourage one from sharing an office with him, if the sexolympics stories didn't. Rumour had it that he'd shot at a fleeing suspect who now wore the slug, stopped by a 2X4, around his neck. Jack was lazy, and his main role in life was hanging around to see if Tina needed him to take over. He'd fulfilled the same role on his last team, and whichever team he was on, if he wasn't on the road, he could be found on the other side of the boss' desk with a newspaper. Jack was hilarious, but sometimes I got the feeling I needed to bring a tape recorder and a lawyer when we worked together. He decided he liked me after we did a liquor seizure on a family of East Indians, in which his primary assistance consisted of theorizing if grandma had been strapped to the roof rack on the way back from Sacramento in order to make room for more Crown Royal.

Lance and Jason were a package deal. Both tall and strapping fellows, they worked as a team. They mostly avoided me. I mostly avoided them. I sensed I was intruding on their turf. As I got to know them better in later years, I got to like one more, and the other less.

Leo and Al were a package deal too. Leo was a nice man, an ex-banker with a singular talent: He could take a five-minute task and extend it into a Russian novel. Al also had a talent, which was bullshitting. He was a rotund Ismaili with a work ethic that made Leo look like a Stakhanovite miner. He sure was good at being a mensch, though. Management loved Al.

Ross was a jock who was lucky to still have a job after a very unfortunate off-duty incident left his head on Internal Affairs' coffee table as a mint tray. He had seven years in when I transferred to Pac, so naturally Tina partnered me up with him, to "keep an eye on him." Luckily, Ross had the good sense to realize he was living a borrowed life, and generally kept his temper in check. Temper is a tough problem for a lot of law enforcement types. We're not supposed to have one, but then we're also supposed to have drive and decisiveness, which in my experience goes hand-in-hand with temper. Temper derails a lot of careers, and I can think of a few times when it almost derailed mine. In the long run, it didn't hurt Ross. He got promoted. Management loves jocks, too.

Julie was an ex-West Yorkshire copper who'd met a Canadian girl and emigrated. Eventually we wound up as partners (the work kind). It was a great match. Where I was the heavy, she was the smooth talker. She played much the same role with me that I was supposed to play with Ross. She reigned me in, which I sometimes desperately needed. She'd also played enough cops and robbers in her time to let me take the lead on stuff I needed to learn. Plus, she kept me laughing. And singing Tom Jones, against my will.

Robyn showed up after I'd been there for a few months. She was tall and striking, and to tell the truth I was a bit intimidated by her. Then I was smitten, but my timing has always been shitty, so nothing ever happened. Robyn wound up with one of the other Bad Boys, Christian, something that I moped about like a twelve-year-old for an inordinate amount of time. She was very smart, so Tina groomed her for management, but like me she had an unfortunate habit of speaking her mind, so that I think that limited her ascent.

Jim showed up after I'd been there about a year. He was destined to be my best friend (poor bastard), but at first, I was a little intimidated by Jim too. First of all, he was from Glasgow, a big bald bastard with an accent so thick I could barely understand what the fuck he was saying half the time. Next, he had sixteen years in corrections, working some truly awful jails in his time, and he effortlessly applied this background to managing people like nobody I'd every worked with. I was a bit jealous about that, and I wasn't the only one. Jack liked to pick at Jim for moving cars slowly. Jim keeps to this day a copy of an e-mail Jack sent him admonishing him for checking people's identifications as they crossed the border. These days, you'll be shot if you don't, but these were different times.

Karina was a hyperactive, skinny Quebecois with a raucous

laugh who had hitchhiked to some very weird places and then wound up with us. It took me a long time to figure out why she was in law enforcement, given her hippie lifestyle (she was living with her boyfriend on a boat when I met her...that was after they'd lived on a bus). But she was actually quite good at cutting through people's horseshit. When I trained her, people called her "Mini-Me," because she...well, you had to be there. Karina was one of those people who would be important in my career right to the end, and she made me laugh. She also could punch harder than any woman I'd ever known.

I didn't know what to make of Dan at first. He was a former Ottawa cop (we seemed to collect ex-cops) with a military bearing and a warped sense of humour. Dan was very smart, and if you argued with him, you'd better know your stuff. He ate eight-dollar chocolate bars and wrote with a six-hundred-dollar pen. If Jack was the team's rotten uncle, Dan was the stern father.

Emilie was a diminutive Montrealer who was so cute that in the team cashier Diane's words, she "Looked like she should be playing with her bike." When I was assigned to train her, I wasn't sure what to expect, but I soon learned that Emilie was a Bad Boy too. Dynamite does come in small packages, after all.

Diane was the team cashier, a sweet and somewhat absent-minded ex-hippie who always made sure we were fed and watered. Coffee runs and donut supply were as much her forte as breaking a fifty, and she took a personal ownership of her kids.

There were eight teams at Pacific Highway then, four teams at a time working rotating shifts at each of the two ports. Douglas, or the "Peace Arch" was a ramshackle old building we'd long since outgrown, in the middle of a Provincial park, with an Indian reservation behind it, a residential neighbourhood and golf course beside it. Down Highway 99 was the US POE. Highway 99 becomes US-5, which runs from Blaine, WA, all the way to Tijuana. There was no shortage of dope on that road. Sometimes we got lucky and found some. We'd work a day-shift rotation, then an afternoon, and then ship over to Pacific Highway Traffic.

Pac Traffic straddles Highway 15, which turns into a truck route that feeds back onto US-5. Next to Pac Traffic is Pac Commercial, a separate port with a separate staff, mostly concerned with searching semi-trailers moving commercial goods. Pac Traffic processed vehicle, foot, and bus traffic. The sound of the bus buzzer, which alerted us to the arrival of another bus in the lane, was a grating irritant. We'd do another two rotations there before doing a night tour with our partner, in which officers from all teams worked together.

Douglas' facilities were antiquated, but it was more fun. The traffic was loopy, the enforcement was better, and the Peace Arch park, looking out over the Pacific Ocean, gave you something nice to look at when nothing was happening. Pac Traffic was surrounded by cargo warehouses and customs brokers, and smell of nearby farms gave it a smell we christened "CAN," or "Cloverdale at Night." So, we preferred Douglas.

Night shifts were not my favourite, but for a number of years I worked them anyway, because the enforcement was good. The craziest fuckers came out at night, and that's when a lot of the best collars got made. But staff was light, and if something happened it was easy to get overwhelmed. Some nights, you did nothing but watch movies. If you worked nights at Pac Traffic, late night buses would keep you hopping until 0200 some nights. They provided the main injection of scum into the Pac Traffic work milieu.

Once I got settled into my team, I began to learn some new things.

NINETEEN

DRUNKS

Of all the realities of the border I needed to get accustomed to, the one that hit me in the face the hardest was this: In 2002, the border was still the Kingdom of the Drunk.

A little history lesson is in order. I already said that Canadians didn't like to spend money in their own country. This applies to getting drunk as well. Bars serving Canadians cheap US booze were a staple of the Washington State economy. In Point Roberts, that little enclave that the map makers forgot, it was even more so. Bars getting Canadians pissed for half what they'd pay at home were almost as important as Tijuana's flat rate booze holes were to Baja California.

My friend Brian, a literate and witty old timer, had many tales of the bad old days, when drunks ran the show. Brian had been at the border since the early 1970s. His brother, Glyn, was a Director in Metro Division.

Brian showed me once the old billy club that had been kept behind the cash desk as a last resort to deal with the drunks, who would act up obnoxiously whenever they were sent into pay taxes on their hooch. The thing had more notches in it than Charles Whitman's sniper rifle.

The secret to taming the drunks? Officer Powers.

Officer Powers referred to the legislation passed in 1999 that gave officers at the border the same powers that frontline police had to deal with things like drunk drivers. Once we were trained and let loose in 2001, with Approved Screening Devices for sampling blood alcohol, and Breathalyzers in many ports, the drunks began to feel the pain.

Cracking down on intoxicated people driving cars across the border was more than just a statistical issue for a lot of officers. In addition to cleaning the offices of foul-mouthed, aggressive pissheads, the hope was that we could prevent more tragedies like the one that unfolded in 1999.

Two 18-year-old girls, best friends, were waiting in the primary line at Douglas when a woman high on prescription drugs and delusionally psychotic plowed into the back of their car at tremendous speed. The officers, including one of my Rigaud classmates on her very first shift, had to watch them burn to death, unable to get near the wreck.

It was not the last time that death would visit the Douglas primary line. And there's no reason to believe Officer Powers would have saved those girls. But cutting into the carnage caused by drunks at the border was a good idea, it seemed to many, including me.

But I had no idea what I was doing. So, I needed to watch the experienced land border officers who did. On Team Five, Lance was the Impaired Driving hotshot, so I made a point of watching him. I learned a few things, relatively quickly.

The first was, take your time. When you suspect someone is driving under the influence, you do not rush to conclusions. You carefully form impressions based on observations. How do they move? Respond to requests and commands? Do they stumble? Stammer?

What can you smell? What do you see in the car? Is there someone else in the car? What do they say? Does a smell of liquor diminish when you get the driver away from the passengers?

There's two ways you can go, legally speaking. Most of the time, border officers lack the lengthy period of observing driving patterns that police officers can engage in on the road. So, skipping the screening device and flat out arresting someone for impaired driving is a rarity at the border. But it's not unheard of. Sometimes, spectacular bad driving does occur, and it's the gateway to a slam-dunk-drunk.

But usually, the Approved Screening Device paves the way. This device is administered by lawful demand, which cannot be refused, absent a lawful excuse. It can be administered in one of three situations, all of which leads an officer to believe the subject is operating a motor vehicle or is in care or control, with alcohol in his or her blood. These circumstances are;

-Admission of consumption: "Sure, I had a couple of beers."
-Odour of liquor on the breath.
-Evidence of consumption in the vehicle (empties).

Wording is everything. You cannot say "odour of alcohol," for instance, because alcohol does not have odour. The impurities in liquor give alcoholic beverages an odour. You must administer demands at the right time, in the right order, for the right reason. You must take careful notes. You must religiously observe each and every step in the process.

In seventeen years at the border, I was involved in many complicated cases, but few cases rivalled an Impaired Driving case for complexity and rigour. The paperwork was stupendous, and took two days, on average, to complete. That was after I knew what I was doing. Rookie impaired files would flounder for weeks.

In the early years, word in the drinking community had not yet gotten around that we could make these demands and administer these tests. So, there was a fair bit more fighting than there needed to be. But that was part of the tenor of the times. Gradually, by clawing our way up the cliffs, a small, hardcore group of border officers became experienced Impaired Driving investigators.

And then, we ran into the courts. Here's a funny fact about Canadian law: There's much more space in the Canadian Criminal Code given over to Impaired Driving than there is to Homicide.

But why, you might ask? Because there are an average of 7-800 murders a year in Canada. Most of these are not whodunits. One of my criminology professors told me about a homicide he attended while working patrol on Vancouver's skid row. The blood trail led from the victim's room to an adjacent room, where the suspect sat cleaning the murder weapon in a sink.

Professor Moriarty, he was not. Doesn't give a lawyer much to work with, does it? Couple that with the fact that most murderers are poor, and it becomes obvious why Impaired Driving law takes up more room in the books.

For starters, there were, before the Provinces started enacting their own, stricter, more effective laws, 50,000 criminal impaired driving cases a year in Canada. These people don't ride the bus. They have money, jobs to lose, and reputations. They can fork over 10,000 bucks for a good lawyer.

And so, lawyers have the economic motivation to get inventive with their defences.

"Your honour, my client was given four chances to blow, not three. The officer must not be confident in his device." (I lost)

"Your honour, the breath technician did not show the mouthpiece to the accused and indicate with his finger where he was to blow." (I lost, despite the accused bragging about how he drove drunk all the time, and drove better that way)

"Your honour, the officer cannot be confident that he checked the calibration date on the device. It is irrelevant that the device's records show it was in working order, if he did not know this." (I lost, after two hours of grilling by a cop turned defence lawyer)

We consoled ourselves by knowing that we had, at least, gotten these menaces off the road. At some great expense to them. And, we learned valuable criminal investigation skills along the way, skills that would help greatly in other areas.

But all too often, the drunks got the last laugh. At least we reminded them that they didn't own the fucking place anymore. And those bars in Point Roberts? My colleagues in Boundary Bay, after some 200 Impaired Driving arrests, shut them down for good.

TWENTY

YOU CLEAR TRAFFIC LIKE OLD PEOPLE FUCK

Generally speaking, the preoccupations of management and the line officers were not the same.

Line staff were generally into getting through their shifts without major aggravation which could impact their careers and/or make them late for dinner/the bar/a hot date. They also, whenever possible, liked to catch bad people doing bad things.

Managers were more concerned with avoiding awkward complaints which might reflect badly on them, and with keeping the traffic moving.

Keeping the traffic moving was, in fact, a national obsession. Over time, this evolved from calling the local radio station with estimated border wait times, to computerized wait time monitoring, and finally, mandatory reporting to Ottawa of any waits in excess of one hour.

But the pressure was always on: keep it moving.

I was astonished when I came from the airport, where checking documents was an obsession, to arrive at a POE where checking ID was considered a pointless nuisance. The dubious concept of "declared citizenship" allowed generations of phonies and cads to skate through border controls. Many people sought in our databases were never checked as a result, and therefore, never caught. Since the agency had never invested in document scanners, and all levels of government were negligent in updating their sometimes shockingly shoddy identification (Indian

Affairs was my favourite; their Status Indian card was less credible than a Blockbuster Video ID), even conscientious checkers like myself could only query a small percentage of IDs we checked.

So, long after 9/11, the border was still pretty much open wide. Officers were typically more interested in invoices and receipts than they were in ID. But they were not the ones to blame.

Ottawa, obsessed with wait times, fought a vicious rearguard action well into the 2000s to keep from having to institute mandatory ID checks. The most scurrilous evidence of this was their reluctance to hook up the national police computer's wants and warrants to the frontline system.

Only after a rapist with an active warrant out for him in Ontario managed to get another visa, and sail back in, uninspected, did the agency cave to public outrage and allow officers to find out on the front line who the actual violent criminals are. In Canada, that is.

I cannot tell you what officers do not yet know on the front line, mostly for security reasons. But I can suggest to you that it is still one hell of a lot. And I can suggest to you only one reason for this state of affairs: The obsession with keeping the traffic moving.

Okay, so keeping it moving is a management obsession. But truth be told, the culture leads officers to internalize this obsession themselves. Put yourselves in our shoes. It's Saturday night, the lineups are pushing one hour, the bosses are pissed, and you've just been assigned another road hour.

Fuck this. You step into the booth, only to hear the FNG you are relieving grilling Gas, Milk, and Cheese people about their last trip to Wuhan. You feel that vein in your head throbbing. And you are tempted to yell, as I did once across three lanes of traffic,

"You clear traffic like old people fuck!"

I mean, come on dude. Keep it moving.

Road hours are dead hours. Only the hopelessly garrulous and completely switched off can look forward to them. If you're meeting management standards, you're doing sixty cars an hour, one car a minute, on average.

There are outliers. I saw a rookie take ten minutes with a car once, then release it. I know a guy who cleared a car in four seconds. Slight problem though: the front seat passenger was dead. Oops.

Most people have nothing interesting to say, and you have no magic questions that will get them to cough it up, unless they give you an opening. That's the fact, Jack. Back when Intelligence was still on the job, we had more confidence that they could pick the wolves from the sheep. But in later years, no amount of front-end grilling was going to sort the nuggets from the sand.

So, roadtimes sucked, unless you got a wrong turn, a nutbar, or someone just not smart enough to keep a secret.

Then, and only then, were roadtimes fun.

TWENTY-ONE

FUN ON THE ROAD

So, I said roadtimes were usually a drag, right? But the unexpected could make it all okay. That one car out of three or four thousand, that makes you break out in a cold sweat, shout "holy fuck!" and go for your gun. Telling the truth here, that's what I lived for.

They sure as fuck were out there.

Let's see, let's see....so many to choose from. Ah, here's a few:

0630 at Douglas, a frosty, dark-as-a-dragon's-colon morning. Single white male who looks like he's been sleeping under overpasses drives up in a VW Jetta with Oregon plates that looks like he just drove it out of a showroom.

"Sir, whose car is this?"

"Um, I don't know."

"Hmm. Well, either you're saying you don't know because you don't want to tell me for some reason, or you really don't know because you stole it. Which is it, then?"

"Ah, I stole it."

"And why did you do that?"

"To get away from the voices in my head."

"Er, step out of the car with your hands where I can see them."

After finding a large ax on the back seat and running the plates through the US NCIC system and finding them clean, I reasoned that Sunshine here might have hacked the owners into tiny bits and taken the car before they could call the five-oh. Luckily, I was only half right. The local sheriffs did a drive by and found the owners sleepy and confused. "Hey, where's our car keys? Where's my ax?"

He wanted to come to Canada and be a lumberjack. Needless to say, work permit denied.

2200 hours, Douglas. The night before Gay Pride begins in Vancouver. I was in the NEXUS lane, where nothing ever happens, and if it does, it's the fucking end of the world. Only cardholders and crazy people go there.

This little fellow was not a cardholder. And he was about to become famous.

One week after the first CBSA officers had been issued firearms, he was about to get one pointed at his empty head. Douglas, as usual, leading the way. Me, whether I like it or not, being present for the shitshow.

"Do you have a NEXUS card, sir?"

(eye twitch) "Nonnnnoooo."

"Then why are you here?"

(more twitching) "Er...to see the things and people. I heard there was a big parade."

"Oh, so you're here for Pride?"

(hateful look) "No."

"Do you have a firearm or weapon in the car, sir?"

(sudden move) "Yes, right here!" With that, he went for the glove box with a cobra's reflexes, causing me to jump out of my chair, unarmed as I still was, and put my R Lee Ermey voice on.

"Don't reach for it! Hands up! Don't move! (calls for backup, begins sweating profusely)

I patted him down with backup, then sent him inside, but only after asking about any more guns. He denied there were any. So, I sent him inside, retrieved and safed a loaded Glock .40 from the glovebox. Then I went inside to see the show.

Inside, my dude was pacing like that Tiger in The Life of Pi. Dan came up beside me. "There's more out there. You ask him?"

"Yup. Gotta be. He said no."

Just then, Katie came into the office and whispered in Chris, the Superintendent and only armed officer's ear. "There's a shotgun in the trunk. And a whole lot of tactical shit, too."

Chris went "Hmm." Then he drew his Beretta PX-4 9mm from his holster and commanded my dude to get on the ground.

I was so stunned that, for the only time in my career, I froze. Dan had to step past me to cuff the guy.

After I got my shit back together, I questioned my weird little dude.

"I'm going to tell you something I've never told anyone else in my career, sir. After looking at the contents of your car; one pistol with magazines, holster, and replacement barrel; one tactical vest and balaclava; one Mossberg tactical shotgun...I am convinced you came here to kill people."

He looked away. "Nnnnnooo."

"That all you got? I mean, you just bought all this stuff! Why did you suddenly acquire this arsenal?"

"Er...I heard noises?"

At that point, I made a decision. I wasn't sure if it was going to be supported, but frankly, I didn't give a fuck. You see, I was thinking back to a story my father had told me about a traffic stop he did on a man named Elery Steven Long, in 1974. He seized a sawn-off shotgun at that time, a weapon he was ordered to give back to Long. My dad refused. His Sergeant gave it back, and a few weeks later Long used that shotgun to kill a Delta Police S/Sgt named Ron McKay.

This is why the Irish breed cops in families, you see. We tell the tales to our sons and daughters. We remember the things they do not teach in a classroom, the way the bandits teach their offspring. To be a second-generation flatfoot is a valuable thing.

I knew the Firearms Act gave me the leverage I needed to keep his guns. So, I kept them. And nobody blinked.

A few years later I read excerpts from my own arrest report in the Canadian Press, as a somewhat garbled version of events made the national news, part of a breathless recounting of times when we'd pulled our guns. *Meta.*

So many times, these interesting encounters start with the words "I don't wanna be here." To an officer, understand, this means, "I've done something wrong, throw me in jail."

Stolen property, stolen cars, loaded guns, kidnapped minors… you name it. Then there's the Wrong Way Jose.

A Wrong Way Jose is an illegal (sorry, "undocumented" alien) who takes a wrong turn, usually under the influence of *mas tequila*, or something stronger. In so doing, he leaves the land of sanctuary policies and enters federal land, where the only thing he has to look forward to is an orange jumpsuit and a bus to Nuevo Laredo.

Like the kid who floored his daddy's pickup, doing 120, high as fuck on meth and wearing Baby Stewie pyjamas, up to my primary booth. Dad came down to see what was up, and he got deported too. Yeah, it's a shame. Laws. You should obey them.

I'm not going to take the last word, here. I'll leave that to my friend Carla.

Carla was a tall and striking brunette with a salty mouth and an unflappable demeanour. She was out in the booth one day when the person she was talking to suddenly disappeared, to be replaced by a fast-talking fucko coming out of a Pontiac Sunfire, claiming to be a cop.

Carla's mind was full of questions, such as; "Why did that guy just get rear-ended?" and "Who is this guy claiming to be a cop, with eight Washington State Troopers pointing carbines, shotguns and tasers at him?" as well as "Why is Cory pointing his gun at this guy?"

"Oh, guess I'd better point my gun at him too." And she did.

TWENTY-TWO
THE BLUE AND THE GREY

Nowadays, everyone in the CBSA is supposed to be one big happy family. The agency that I spent most of my career working for was actually only formed in 2003, as an amalgamation of Customs, Immigration, and Food Inspection.

Yes, because all those things go together so well.

In some ways, of course, integration made sense. Or it should've, but remember always that the first rule of bureaucracy is take any solution, then calmly fuck it into a cocked hat. We did all work at the same crossings, dealing with the same people, and it made sense for us to talk to each other without constraints. Theoretically, we could save on management overhead, but then we just went ahead and made a whole bunch of new managers anyway.

But in other ways, integration was a Frankenstein's monster. There existed two very distinct cultures at the border, the Immigration culture (Grey), and the Customs culture (Blue).

Food Inspection? I laugh. In the years before integration, we never saw those guys at the land border. And after, we produced generations of recruits convinced of how deadly serious it was to keep Washington State apples out of BC. Apparently it was never serious enough before to warrant anyone actually driving to the border. But I digress.

Immigration people worked out of their own office, co-located at the POE, enforcing the strange and byzantine world of Immigration law. Immigration law seemed to come with a great many clauses like, "This shall be the case, unless it is Tuesday." I never learned to understand it, but, unfortunately, after integration, it became the tail that wagged the giant dog. Slowly, Immigration culture, the Grey Goo, would take over the agency.

This was a problem for guys like me because Immigration culture was a largely passive, historically oriented, client-service focused business. Grey people would sit at the counter, inches from a person with a savagely violent criminal record, questioning them calmly about each atrocity, without ever thinking to ask, "Hey, does this guy have a gun on him *right now*?"

That was if they checked in the computer. There was one old-timer named Robert who prided himself on his ability to get the truth from anyone, without silly things like verification. Robert would sit there in his cardigan sweater and chit-chat with monsters adorned with prison tats, then calmly release them, proclaiming them pure and without sin.

Some of us Blue types got in the habit of running our own checks first, then delivering the stack of bad news to the Grey types, so we all understood each other. That put people like Robert in a tough spot.

It was much easier to monitor the hijinks of the Grey ones at Pac Traffic than it was at Douglas. At Douglas, the Customs and Immigration offices were separated by 100 metres of corridor known as the Glass Alley. If you didn't make sure your Immigration referral went to Customs first, some dubious things could happen.

Usually, these dubious things were as a result of laziness, or simple Garbage-In-Garbage-Out programming. A tremendous amount of computer hits on people were the result of a single interaction resulting in an "Allowed to Leave" document being issued to a person, which resulted in a scarlet letter on their name, for life. Many of these ATLs were for very trivial matters, such as a person applying for a permit without the right documents, but unfortunately removing them from the antiquated Immigration computer system took time.

Only Customs officers worked the road, so we continually referred the same people for nothing, and Immigration released them. So, who would look like the bad guy? Soon, the officers who never checked ID began to look like they were onto something.

One day, one of my colleagues saw something much more interesting happening with one of his referrals. Ajit was a tall brown guy with a big nose, a thick working-class British accent, and an endless supply of jokes. He was a serial workplace dater at the time, and one of his former girlfriends was on duty at the other end of the glass alley when Ajit sent in an American man as a name hit.

After his hour was up, he walked down to the Immigration office in time to see the American being escorted out of the office by Ajit's ex, who then planted a kiss on the man, and let him drive up the road. Ajit watched, speechless for once, then reported what he'd seen. It turned out that the man was criminally inadmissible and had been let go many times by this same officer. She was fired.

Another substantial difference in Immigration vs Customs culture was in our attitudes towards use of force. Yes, the Grey ones had vests, and belts with weapons and cuffs on them, but they typically kept those hung up in the office while they interacted with people through plexiglass. When rough stuff erupted in their office, we were often called down to sort it out. One day, we entered the Immigration office to search a man we suspected of having a gun on him. We did our business and let him go, but we'd put some noses out of joint.

At Team Five's next staff meeting, our guest of honour was the Immigration Manager, who proceeded to give us holy shit for

"Boosting" one of their "clients" in their office. Whereupon a few of us responded that we'd "boost" their "client" in his *private* office if we thought he had a gun on him.

There were some tensions, is what I'm saying.

But it wasn't all bad. We had our favourites among the Grey ones, people who seemed to get that their job was to protect Canadians first, not the "clients." We liked these Immigration officers, people like the spousal duo of Denise and Norm, the veteran Jim W, and later arrivals such as Ruby and Sarb.

And as we started having to enforce Immigration laws ourselves, we began to understand that there was a great gap between what we thought should happen, and what actually could happen, given the confusing and often contradictory legislation we had to work with. Blue and Grey were not necessarily so Black and White, after all.

And, as experienced Immigration types began to take early retirement, not at all thrilled with the prospect of doing road hours and searching cars, people who actually knew how to do complicated things like process refugee claims became rarer and rarer. We began to value their expertise more than we had before.

And, as Blue culture changed, we began to see how some of "ours" could make decisions every bit as shitty as those made in the old Grey days.

I remember working primary one day when a huge truck towing a massive trailer arrived in my lane. The driver and sole occupant was a middle-aged white guy with a confident smile. He must've been towing all of his belongings. He told me he was headed to Kelowna, a city in the Interior, about four hours away.

Then he handed me an American passport with an expired Temporary Resident Permit inside. "I'm here to get a new one." He assured me confidently. "I've got all my paperwork."

Temporary Resident Permits, or TRPs, are supposed to be issued to foreign nationals who are inadmissible to Canada, but whose entry would be inadvisable for one of only two reasons:

1. Significant Benefit to Canada
2. Humanitarian and Compassionate Grounds

In practice, some officers get a little TRP-happy. It's always easier to be the nice guy who finds a way to please a "client" than it is to slam the door in their face. "Significant Benefit" is really supposed to mean "Guy has a DUI, but he's the only person who fix a machine that 300 people's jobs depend on." In practice, it can easily become "Guy has two assaults, but he spent a lot of money on this fishing charter, and he's always wanted to see Canada."

I noticed that I was looking at a serious criminality TRP, which could only be authorized by a Chief. "What do you need this for?"

"First degree child rape." He answered with a smirk, as if we were talking about jaywalking. I decided immediately that I would take a very malevolent interest in his case.

"Okay then." I filled out a referral card with a giant code for "call me first" on it and sent him in.

Sarb called me. "Don't worry. He's not getting it. No way."

"I figured you'd say that." Sarb was a mother of three who had no time for sex offenders. "Do me a favour and find me the file? I'd like to see who gave him one in the first place, and why."

Maybe it was none of my business, but I took a personal interest in the cross-border movement of sex offenders. American sex offenders loved Canada. We didn't have the same sort of draconian restrictions on their movements or residency, and we didn't make them go door-to-door announcing, "Hi, I'm Tim, your new neighbour, and I'm a baby raper."

The file was big. Our "client," by then on his way home with his tail between his legs, had shacked up with a woman in Kelowna who had two boys, aged four and three. He'd been convicted on raping his own eight-year-old daughter. In my experience, that's rare. Even most sex-offenders don't touch their own biological kids.

But he had. Full genital penetration. It was an unpleasant read, to say the least. But apparently, it was all good! The baby-raper had brought a report from his own shrink, assuring us that his client was low risk to reoffend. But he was still sexually attracted to kids. That was the small print.

The examining officer, a management favourite who was now at HQ in Ottawa, had recommended the TRP be issued, based on the psychologist's report, and on Humanitarian and Compassionate grounds. The "client" needed to be with his girlfriend and *her children!*

The Chief agreed and signed off on it. No demand for another, independent report. No move to take the case to a hearing. No consideration of the who the real "client" might be. Canada's children, perhaps? Specifically, a four and three-year-old in Kelowna?

Cases like this made me realize what I hated about Immigration work. If you didn't keep focus on the big picture, the VERY big picture, it was easy to lose track of right and wrong. Too many officers, Grey, Blue, integrated, had fallen, and would continue to fall into the trap of looking at the person standing in front of them as the only one whose needs had to be considered.

In some ways, it was easier to be Blue. It was very hard to consider the person in front of you a "client" if you held the tangible evidence of their crimes, instead of a computer printout, in your hands.

People who think a border officer's job is easy have no fucking clue. They have no idea of the countless forces pushing and pulling you to say "yes," instead of the far less popular "no."

Maybe that's why I never liked the term "Border *Services* Officer." It confuses people, who, unlike me and some others, do not think of themselves as the border *police.*

Grey or Blue, it is the police's job to protect the innocent, not service "clients." It may seem like an exercise in semantics, but in this case, semantics are important.

Officers who believe their clients are innocent children will never allow child rapists into a home with Canadian children. And that's as important as semantics ever get.

TWENTY-THREE

COCAINE HIGHWAY

Before everything got all...integrated, the mission, the big obsession of the majority of the officers was getting dope.

BIG dope, that is. Everyone knew that dope was pouring across the border. So much cocaine was coming up the US-5 from Mexico that BC, 10,000 kilometres from the nearest coca plant, was becoming a net EXPORTER of cocaine.

Clearly, we hadn't done much to blunt the supply. And demand? That wasn't our problem, but it was obvious that, while we tried to dent supply, other forces were placating demand. This was the era when drug users were forming unions, crack pipes were being handed out, and open street-level dealing was being ignored, just 30 kilometres north of where we tried to interdict the pure stuff.

What was the point, again?

But in those days, I hadn't really gotten that cynical yet. Finding dope was the name of the game. We had a small cadre of experienced intelligence officers, who were widely respected both inside and outside of the agency. We had a Flexible Response Team (FRT), dedicated to targeted enforcement, who acted as both inspiration and competition to the rest of us.

We had a chance of getting good dope seizures. Frontline officers were still trusted with good intelligence and stamping out immigration permits had not yet become our primary rationale.

But it was still really, really, really fucking hard to get dope. By this time, serious smuggling operations had learned to recruit people who aroused less suspicion, and/or equipped them with such good concealment that it didn't matter how suspicious we were.

Many hours-long, exhausting examinations ended with an "I'm sure there was dope in there. We just weren't smart enough to find it."

One example of the people smuggling groups were using to run circles around us was a case from Huntington, out in the Valley. A 65-year old man was crossing every week to "put flowers on my son's grave." Only when a brand-new student officer grilled him was he finally caught with a load of cocaine.

Concealment, deep concealment within the body of the vehicle, was more often than not the way we got beaten. Only occasionally did we trip over someone who had no clue or had just gotten lazy. My friend Cecilia caught a woman once who had gotten so blasé about drug smuggling that she simply put ten kilos in a duffel bag and dropped it behind her driver's seat. But that was the exception, not the rule.

Smuggler inventiveness forced us to up our game. Intelligence officers, most notably Paul, a Kiss fan with a computer-bank knowledge of mechanical concealment, became recognized experts in the field of deep smuggling.

Anybody with access to an autobody shop could build a false compartment. Some favourite areas were the beds of pickup trucks and cargo areas of vans and SUVs. Bigger vehicles on the road meant more room for dope.

Compartments ran from the crude to the sophisticated. Sometimes the "compartment" was just a natural void in the structure of a vehicle. Sometimes it was an elaborate, Rube Goldberg contraption, involving strange fuse settings, magnetic locks, particular switch settings, and hydraulic actuators.

We would receive intelligence on the more advanced work of our American colleagues, and despair. I could barely change a tire. How the fuck was I supposed to find dope inside a transmission shaft? While other officers blithely spoke of dropping gas tanks and disconnecting this, that, and the other thing, I would always wonder how the fuck I'd ever put it back where it was supposed to be.

As Dirty Harry said, "A man's got to know his limitations." Eventually I took that to heart. I was good at profiling, questioning, and everyday drug recognition. That was my passport to bigger and better things. As so often at the border, the secret wasn't so much what you could do as an individual, but who you teamed up to do it with.

I chipped away, doing small dope and cash seizures, learning more, building certain working assumptions that I would retain throughout my career. These were:

1. Smuggling groups would all love to get grandma to work for them, but grandma rarely wants to. Most people who smuggle drugs are like polished turds. They might look good from a distance, but dig a little, and you'll find someone you'd expect.
2. People who smuggle drugs often use drugs. They need the money, and they'll give off all the signs of a casual or addicted user. Don't discount them. I once got an exam handed off to me by an FRT member. She'd caught a hippie type tossing a mint tin into the trash. "It's just hash." She asked me, "Do you want it?" Actually, it was black tar heroin, and 30,000 USD in drug money with a goldmine of intelligence. The harmless hippie was a smack dealer. With a very helpful ledger. I believe I sent the FRT member chocolates. They look like hash, too.

3. Money and guns go nicely with drugs. Don't categorize. Most crooks are omnivores. Mike, a veteran dog handler, performed one of the most difficult tasks possible in our work when he popped a drug swallower. This guy was full stem to stern. He got his start smuggling fireworks, then moved on to booze. Liars are liars.
4. Can't find it? Get a second opinion. Years later, after my biggest seizure ever, I saw the exact same model car sitting in secondary. I walked into the office and found Trevor and Sukh in Jessie's office. Trevor was the undisputed king of cold hit dope seizures, who taught deep concealment searches at our training facility in Chilliwack. Sukh was a talented junior officer. Jessie was my Superintendent. They were at that last gasp moment, one I'd been at so many times, when you are wondering, "What the fuck are we missing?" I casually pointed out where James, Mike and I had found the dope last time. Trevor could've been an arrogant dick about it, but that's not the way he was wired. They went back out there and pulled a couple of kilos. Give your ego a rest, and work as a team.

One chilly night in December 2005, I got a chance to put all of my theories to work. Mad Dog was the Superintendent that night. I was on overtime, and I'd switched for a regular booth with Gorav, a laconic junior officer with tremendous incipient talent. But Gorav would be kicking himself for taking a NEXUS time, because I was about to hit one out of the park.

Mad Dog was an old-timer with a few screws loose. He was known for stealing people's lunches, and if you really wanted to argue something with him, he'd win the argument by producing a pie chart or a line graph. He once listened to a lengthy traveler complaint, seeming to take notes the whole time. But when the traveler finished, Mad Dog turned it around:

SHIT HAPPENS

"Hey, Patterson, Mike's got the dog out now, so send a few in for him, eh?"

"Fine, Mad Dog."

My first couple amounted to nothing. But then Zamora drove up. I can use his real name because he was convicted in a court of law and sent to prison. Zamora showed me an American passport showing his birthplace in Chile. He was going to hang out with somebody in a hotel, a suitably vague reason for visiting. He seemed to think that I ought to be impressed that he was a merchant seaman. The car was a shitbox Chrysler.

There's profiling, then there's profiling. He's from Chile. Most people from Chile don't smuggle drugs. But it's in the neighbourhood, and he speaks the language of coca. He's a merchant seaman, a guy who can easily get things on and off ships. Plus, his car would never be missed if the government seized it.

When I handed him his referral slip and told him to pull over, he gave me a look like "There must be some mistake." But he went in anyway.

He had the bad luck to encounter James, who as we've already established is the last officer you want to run into in this situation. He tried to play the big shot, but that doesn't work with James. By the time I got off the road, he was cowed, sitting and staring at the ceiling.

"I've got a good feeling about this one." James said. "There's a CPIC hit for a guy named 'Samora' for trafficking out of Montreal."

"Bet it's him. Montreal always fucks up warrants."

"Wanna come look at the car?"

"Let's do it."

James took the passenger side; I took the drivers. Patting down the seatback, I immediately felt lumps where there should be no lumps. I found the zip and pulled. Two plastic and tape-wrapped kilo bricks fell onto the floor. James looked at me, wide-eyed, as another brick fell out on his side.

I've never seen a man's face turn grey. But Zamora's face turned grey when we hooked him up. Mike joined us and showed us how to take apart the rear passenger compartment. In the void between the trunk and the back seat, we found the bulk of the 30 kilos.

The CPIC entry was him, and he was already wanted for smuggling in Montreal. He was the western anchor of a smuggling group Intel and the Mounties would later roll up, with six other members moving over a ton of cocaine from Long Beach, California, to Vancouver, to Montreal. The gang was straight out of a Guy Ritchie film, being run by a Chilean transsexual.

He was on his 24th trip. He got seven years in prison, then he was deported.

James and I got two-sentence letters on our files as our reward from the Chief. They weren't even on letterhead, for fuck's sake. But they can never take the thrill of scoring cold dope away from me. There's only one case I'm prouder of, and that one was far in the future.

TWENTY-FOUR

THOSE WHO CAN'T

After three or four years on the job, I began to fancy that I knew a few things. This is always a dangerous time in a young officer's career.

As Donald Rumsfeld was saying right around the same time, while he was massively fucking up a war, "We don't know what we don't know." Which is exactly the problem a still-junior officer has.

He or she has seen a fair bit, depending on where they've been working. But it's a fair assumption they haven't seen it all. They may think they have, though.

Though the CBSA has some very busy ports, the ones in Pac District among them, there is no real analogue to the situation in a big city police department. In Vancouver City, or Surrey RCMP, for example, there *are* places where two or three years of patrol work will give the young cop a general smorgasbord of almost everything the job has to offer.

Pac District could be intense. But it wasn't *that* intense.

Right around this time, I began to steer into some avoidable potholes. Complaints I could have avoided, but I just had to put that one extra sentence in. I still hadn't learned one thing I would later come to believe almost religiously: You can't fix people's attitudes. If people are stupid and ignorant, they've probably been that way for a long time. They think it's okay, and they don't want to change. If anyone's going to change that, it might be a spouse or a minister; it sure as shit won't be you.

As my dad liked to say, "Write the ticket, or give the lecture. Don't do both."

Historically, this was a good time to absorb this lesson. After a couple of years of "tightened" security following 9/11, the powers that be had decided to bring back expedited clearance.

Expedited clearance programs catered to people who had to cross the border frequently. Remember, the people with the sense of entitlement? Well, NEXUS was perfect for them. For fifty dollars, the self-appointed diplomat could cruise past the lineups for five years.

Of course, there were rules. At first, they were strict, but the old-timers had shaken their heads and muttered, "It won't last." And indeed, it didn't. Over the course of ten years, exceptions to the rule spread into a giant chasm of no rules. Fifty dollars for five years began to buy a sort of diplomatic immunity.

I saw a perfect indication of this early on. I was at the temporary POE at Douglas, the old eyesore having been torn down for the coming Olympics. I heard the port siren sound, and ran outside the building to see a man calmly driving the wrong way down the freeway, flashing a NEXUS card at me as if it were a badge.

People like this like to complain. I began to avoid NEXUS, sensing no matter how quiet the roadtimes, it wasn't worth the trouble. People were coming through the lane with fucking pianos strapped to the roofs of their vans, insisting they had "Nothing to declare." Chutzpah doesn't begin to cover it.

In the NEXUS booth at Douglas, an officer had succinctly underlined the problem. They'd drawn on the windowsill the word "LIARS" with an arrow pointing to the traveler.

Of course, this wasn't true of all, or even most of them. But officers do love to generalize.

With the expectation of expedited clearance came the expectation of zero wait times, and zero questions. Tina had given me a rare chance to fill in for her at Pac Traffic, and I was wearing the stripes when I went out to inspect the line.

Jim was out there, and he'd just released a traveler who'd peeled his little car crazily into secondary. "What's his problem?"

Jim chuckled. "Oh, he was comparing my lineup with Mike's over there." Next to Jim, a student officer was firing them out like a machine gun. Nothing bothered me like someone who got fast before they got good. "He said it was a scientific impossibility for my line to be slower than the other."

"Oh, he's a scientist, is he?" I returned to the office to find Al schmoozing with the grumpy old man. "Thanks Al. I've got this."

"But..." I knew Al was apologizing on behalf of the Queen, as we said, but I was never any good at that.

"Thank you, Al. There's a lineup at the counter. Well sir, I'm Acting Superintendent Patterson. What's the issue today?"

The guy proceeded to outline his theory of border lineups, and why Jim was worse than Hitler for asking him four questions. He was part of a peculiar species of old white guys we loved to cater to at the border. We catered to them, in my opinion, by doing the kind of ass kissing Al specialized in.

I was more a fan of Mad Dog's approach. I put up a hand. "Sir, I have heard you out here, and there's one thing I'd like you to consider."

"What's that?"

"Well sir, border officers are supposed to be vigilant, and protect Canada's security and economy. They do this by asking questions. Since the officer in your lane was asking more questions, do you think it's possible he was actually doing a better job?"

This was an entirely rhetorical question.

The man stammered. "Well...but...well, then why wasn't the other guy doing his job?"

I smiled condescendingly. "Sir, who do you want to complain about now?"

"Uh...I don't know?"

I took out my business card. "Sir, I have reviewed your complaint, and I have found it invalid. If you disagree with this decision, please write the Administrative Superintendent at this address. Have a super day!"

He walked out, muttering. I think I would've made a good Superintendent. Not everyone might agree.

All of this got me thinking about field training the new recruits. Traditionally, field training was sink or swim. New recruits were now arriving directly from the make-believe environment of Rigaud, then they were passed around like a bowl of potato chips to catch as catch can.

They learned good things, and bad. On some teams, they learned nothing but bad habits. On others, like ours, they did learn mostly good habits. So, Julie and I put the case to Tina for a formalized program, to hold trainers, recruits, and supervisors accountable for a recruit's progress, or lack thereof.

My dad had been one of the RCMPs first Recruit Field Trainers, so I naturally had an interest. At first, it was fun. I got people with natural talent and energy, like Karina and Emilie. In later years, it got harder, as hiring standards were adjusted, and recruits developed a greater sense of entitlement.

But I realized how much I enjoyed teaching, and as I began to get a bit burned out, I started thinking the previously unthinkable.

Rigaud was looking for Facilitators, to train new recruits. Maybe I would be riding the Magic Schoolbus again.

TWENTY-FIVE

GUNS

Aside from drunks, another elephant in the room at every border POE was the gun.

Their guns, that is. We did not yet carry guns, and when I arrived at the border, the current President of the CBSA, a meteorologist named Alain Jolicoeur, had declared that we would get guns "over my dead body."

Mr Jolicoeur publicly self-destructed during a press conference after the Dziekanski Incident at Vancouver Airport. He thought he could limit the media to five questions, and they would obey meekly, like the people he bossed around in Ottawa. This simply reinforces my belief, long held, that having letters after your name in no way makes you smart. Oh, by the way, this was two years after the firearms program for the CBSA was announced. So much for fighting to the death, eh Al?

He is now the Vice-Chair of the Board of Governors for the University of Ottawa, a perfect settling perch for members of the Laurentian Elite who have fucked things up in the civil service too much to be of use to even a Liberal government.

On his University of Ottawa bio-page, the word "border" is misspelled.

Basically, I spent the early years of my career working for a weatherman, which says a lot about why the CBSA perpetually rides the short bus of law enforcement. Bosses hated arming, not because they had analyzed it dispassionately and found it made no sense, but because they were cloistered academics who did not like things that made loud noises.

So, we were tasked with controlling the flow of firearms from the most heavily armed civil society on earth, where firearms ownership is enshrined in the constitution, armed with nothing more than a policeman carries in practically gunless Britain.

To give you some perspective on the problem, consider that, in 2012, 11% of the adult population of Washington State had a permit to carry a concealed firearm. That's not a permit to own a firearm, or carry one in your vehicle; no, that's a permit to carry one on your person.

Granted, not all, or even most of these people exercised this right while crossing the border. But there was a large enough minority who did not possess such good sense, especially when factoring in the populations of US states further from Canada, to whom the idea of "leave your guns at home" made as much sense as "learn Hungarian now." These people mainly arrived in the summer.

Given this fact, it was amazing to me, and my retired cop father, that we did not carry guns. I came to regard this, after more and more close calls, as a fundamental threat to my life. So many of the people we dealt with had guns, yet we did not. The agency blithely assured us that, if we needed them, the police were close by. Yet I always remembered the aphorism favoured by American gun owners:

"When seconds count, the police are minutes away."

As my dad had taught me, when I had down time, I'd run through possible scenarios involving people who did not meekly go along with arrest and seizure of their guns, but who decided to fight. The happy outcome of such scenarios always relied on either a Mountie just happening to be in the office at the time, or a lucky gun grab.

Luck is not preparation. Perhaps they didn't cover that in weatherman school.

Our training was awkwardly silent on the subject of weapons in general. If we encountered a scenario which "exceeded the limits of our training and ability," we were to "withdraw." The exact technique for "withdrawing" from a person with a loaded gun pointed at us was never discussed in detail.

Frankly, I figured "withdrawal" was a not particularly reliable method of birth control, and an even less reliable method of self-defence. Yet, we continued reporting for duty with no deadly force options save trust in the almighty.

It wasn't as if we didn't know the risk was there. It certainly was, but the agency and our political masters went to great lengths to conceal it. A union official in Ontario had complied a list of over 250 recent assaults and armed attacks on officers and was harassed for his troubles.

Events in our area had included a gangbanger from LA, who after his arrest for smuggling a handgun proclaimed, "Shit, if I knew you muthafuckers was unarmed, I'd have wasted you." Another situation involved a former US Army Special Forces soldier who surprised a female officer searching his car, took his handgun back from her, then engaged in a struggle with her backup officer. Had Andre not had the presence of mind to press the magazine release during the fight, unloading the pistol, we could very well have lost two officers that day. Other ports had officers taken hostage at gunpoint, an officer shotgunned at primary, and countless other knife-pulls, bottle-smashes, vehicular assaults, and sinister threats and stalking.

Someone was going to get killed, it was only a matter of time. So far, all of my gun seizures had been compliant. Most Americans we seized guns off of were not criminals per se; they were simply ignorant, like many of their countrymen, of the fact that other countries also had laws, and there were consequences for not obeying them.

It did not help matters that our enforcement at the time acted as little deterrent: most gun smugglers were not criminally prosecuted.

The situation worried me and Jim enough that we eventually joined a large group of officers across the country in filing a union grievance against being forced to work unarmed. A few months later, we were summoned to the Chief's office for a response.

Everything's fine, came the party line. Nobody needs guns. Were we satisfied with this?

"Hell no." We replied in unison. But soon, our grievance would become irrelevant. Politics would overtake events, and our union would make the unarmed frontier a campaign issue.

The Conservatives, looking for another issue to make the governing Liberals look bad on, couldn't have chosen a better one. After all, the Liberals had a recent minister who'd maintained we were essentially bank tellers, and if we were such whiny babies about our safety, we could have those little buttons the tellers pressed to bring the real police. Such buttons were actually installed in the new Douglas POE.

We begged to differ. Officers in Ontario began to shut down ports with safety complaints over "Armed and Dangerous" border crossers. The spectre of jammed supply routes and shutdown auto plants began to haunt Ottawa. The Liberals backtracked, now promising to permanently deploy police to babysit us (imagine how bored they'd be), but it was too late.

The Conservatives won with a decent minority. On the second day they were in office, the new bosses announced a hefty pay raise for us, and armed officers as soon as 2007. We rejoiced at finally being out from under the Liberal heel.

Just after the election, we were reminded that we'd made getting guns a priority just in time. Two murder suspects from California were apprehended inches from the border by US Customs. The US agents, aware that their unarmed Canadian colleagues were sitting ducks, executed a daring shoot-and-ram operation that stopped them within a literal hair's breadth of the border.

We got lucky, again, with a little help from our friends. But that luck would not last forever.

TWENTY-SIX

CHANGES

The changes at the beginning of 2006 were big for me personally, and not just for my job.

For one thing, I was on my way to longer being single. In January, I met my then-online girlfriend Diana, a former Ford model who ran a company that did laser light shows for special events. My relatives were quick to point out that she looked like Catherine Zeta-Jones, which she in fact sort of did. Don't ask me why she picked me. She wasn't even looking for a PR card. I had to convince her to move here.

I had my first exposure to the Southern hemisphere in the mind-blowing megalopolis of Sao Paulo, Brazil, where Diana lived. It was hot, and loud, and vast, a full-on assault on the senses. The beef was amazing, the caipirinha cocktails were better, and the women...well, that was what I was there for, anyway.

Hooked on Diana and Brazil, I knew I was going to be doing a lot of traveling. One thing that made working in Rigaud so attractive. See, when you're posted to Rigaud as a "Facilitator" (instructor is not PC enough, apparently), you get paid for incidentals, despite the fact that your rent and meals are basically either spoken for or so cheap it doesn't bear mentioning.

Essentially, you walk away every month with not two, but three, paycheques. And the third one is tax-free, baby.

You've gotta love the civil service. Yes, we're leeches. But if you could, you'd be sucking away too, like you were trapped inside

Catherine Zeta-Jones' sweater.

I traded the heat of Sao Paulo in January for the ice world of Quebec in February.

I thought I was ready, but I really wasn't. This time it was colder, or I was older, or a combination of the two. *Minus fucking twenty-five.* Take a breath, freeze your head. I had a bigger room this time, and it was harder to get fired, but it was still Rigaud, and Operation Mind Fuck was still in effect.

Sure, it was easier. There were some good people I got to know out there, like Calgary Jim, a wisecracker and big mouth like me. Holly was from Vancouver Airport, and once stole a fellow facilitator's handi-capable scooter, then went back and forth in front of her class doing the "beep beep" routine from Austin Powers. I knew Renee from the airport days too.

There was also Kitten. Funny how in a big job, in a huge country, you can meet people you click with only once, and never see them again. And then, like Kitten, you can meet people you sincerely vow never to meet again, and keep bumping into them, over and over. I was convinced that if I were somehow posted to Mercury, I'd run into Kitten's smirking face.

It was the smirk, yes, but it was also the seemingly bottomless urge to please the bosses that irked me so about Kitten. I'd last spent any significant time around him back in 2001, bumped into him a few times at Pac, but when I went back east in 2006, he was on his way to becoming a big wheel.

People like Kitten go far. They are already performing an act, so censoring themselves is no harder than asking a Shakespearean actor not to sub gangsta rap for King Lear. When their recruits point out that this shit you're teaching doesn't make sense, sir, you just come back a flip reply, of which he had many.

As I settled in, I quickly realized two things: One, there was an in-crowd, and an out-crowd, and I was in the out-crowd.

The in-crowd got to teach cool things, regardless of whether they'd ever done those things in the field. People from Ottawa Air Cargo were teaching Impaired Driving investigation. Why? They had a certificate that said they could.

One thing that never changed in the years I spent in the CBSA was their damn-near religious certainty that you could teach anyone to do anything, provided you sent them on the right course. I was sure that if the agency needed to produce fugu chefs, or Soviet nuclear reactor operators, it would shamelessly do so, and supply the requisite certificates.

I had arrested lots of impaired drivers, but I got to teach making tax entries, and filling out forms. I had to weasel my way into teaching more interesting things or find a way to make boring stuff interesting. I did like a challenge.

The second thing I found out quickly: There was a lot of fucking down time.

Back in 2006, down time was not as much fun as it is now. There were no smart devices, and our computers could access no site more exciting than the CBC. So, Jim and I spent a lot of time in our shared office coming up with interesting pen arrangements on our desks, or making sticky notes into puzzles, that sort of thing.

I had lots of time to send e-mails to Diana. And look out the window and wonder, "Is it too cold to go to the Metro and get more booze?"

Gradually, I carved out my little niche. I taught the boring shit, with a smile on my face, and tried mightily to make it interesting. I found a few courses nobody else wanted to teach that I very much did. I taught recruits how to fill out enforcement paperwork, which allowed my scope to tell enforcement stories, which my recruits loved hearing, in large part because most of the other facilitators had no stories to tell. I taught drug testing, which allowed for lots of butt-smuggling and junkie stories. But my favourite was CBRNE.

The government loves acronyms. One of my recruits invented one herself, which was "NMA," or "No More Acronyms." CBRNE stood for "Chemical, Biological, Radiological, Nuclear, Explosives." It was a rather shameless attempt by HQ to fit what should be a one-week counter-terrorism course in four hours (cute detector dog demonstrations permitting).

The bare bones of CBRNE were as boring as a bureaucrat could make a porno film. Which is to say, boring as fuck. But there was so much room for a cool course there, that I spent less and less time competing with Jim's prodigious pen-arranging skills, and more time trying my hand at curriculum design.

My mom was a teacher. What can I say, it was as much in my blood as arresting people.

Curriculum design was tricky. Very few changes were allowed. So, my attempt to convert the course into a discussion of terrorists, not just the weapons they used, was largely unsuccessful.

I kept on talking about what I wanted to talk about anyway. I loved it. I'm a weapons of mass destruction nerd, a condition brought about by months of off-topic reading when I was in university. In those days, I actually learned how to at least describe how to make a nuclear bomb, something I hadn't thought was actually possible earlier.

But the knowledge was out there, and that got me thinking: who the fuck else is reading this shit?

As far as the CBSA was concerned, this was not a merely academic question. In 1998, officers at Beaver Creek on the Alaskan border had intercepted a white supremacist with a bag of white powder. When they went to open the bag, Hitler Junior just about hit the ceiling. Now, if you ask me, that should have been a clue something was wrong. But the officers sealed the bag in the Superintendent's safe, where it sat for two years.

Whether the subject was drug testing or CBRNE, I always tried to tell the recruits: *context is everything.* Ordinarily, a bag of white powder is an invitation to a drug test. But if you're dealing with a skinheaded incest poster boy whose favourite conversational topic is "Why we should kill all the Jews," you might want to pause. Opening that bag could cost you your life.

Sitting in that safe at Beaver Creek was enough ricin to put Canada in violation of the Biological Weapons Treaty. Oh, and kill half the population from Vancouver to Toronto. So, I figured CBRNE was a worthwhile pursuit.

For a while, I was happy in my little niche. I had good students. Trips to Montreal and Ottawa. Interesting stuff to teach, or at least, stuff I'd made interesting to teach. And I was socking away that incidental money for my next Brazil trip.

But happiness never lasts. Especially in the CBSA. I was about to become a marked man.

TWENTY-SEVEN
ARE THESE PEOPLE ON DRUGS?

I was supposed to spend a year in Rigaud. In March, that certainly seemed doable.

I was spending most of my time with the recruits of Class-202, a diverse bunch that included Army Guy, a…well…army guy. Bobbi, a transplanted Newfie with a better ability to quote movie lines, and a more warped sense of humour than mine. Cowboy, a backwoods BC boy with the ability to sidestep any complaints about the shit that came out of his mouth with the defence that he just found the whole thing so baffling. And Jane, a gorgeous Toronto girl who seemed to understand every aspect of the mind fuck. Did I mention she was gorgeous?

They were a good bunch. Almost every one of them was interesting, and after we lost one on D-1, I was determined to keep the rest. I became almost, paternal, you might say.

They were my kids, and I intended to keep them together till the end. Even the ones who hadn't yet learned how to raise their voices, straighten their backs, and show some goddamned command presence. I would fucking teach them.

But the system conspired against such straightforward thinking. One cold day in March, I was out watching D-1 simulations when one of my recruits asked me, in all seriousness, about the actors: "Are these people on drugs?"

I hummed and hawed, but I could not really say "no." I wondered the same thing.

In the intervening five years, the cadre of actors who staffed the scenario-based training at Rigaud had gotten no better. In fact, they had gotten quite entrenched, with the connivance of the senior facilitators, who in my opinion, had begun to forget that these were, after all, contractors we were talking about.

Calgary Jim showed me a video that made me quite concerned. "You're not gonna fucking believe this." He said, before bringing me into a private room. "I wasn't sure who I should show this to, so I figured I'd come to you first. Watch this."

Bridget was one of the better recruits from another class, a young woman with fairly unflappable calm. In the video, she was practising a baggage exam for her D-2 test. The one I'd botched five years before. She was squared off against one of the actors, who apparently had decided that today was her day to experiment with the Stanislavsky Method. She objected to being searched by screaming and tossing everything out of her suitcase at Bridget. Followed by the suitcase.

"Is she on drugs?" Jim asked.

Bridget responded by calmly taking out her notebook and informing the actor that she was under arrest for Hindering an Officer.

"Good for her." I said.

"They didn't think so. They told her it wasn't an arrest scenario." Jim shook his head. "What the fuck are we teaching these kids?"

"So, what do you want to do?"

"I was thinking of bringing it up in the next Facilitators meeting. Will you back me up?"

"Yeah." I agreed. What else could I say?

In the meantime, we had a bit of fun. Brian and I used a bit of down time to set up a deep concealment scenario training session. We loaded two old junkers full of hides, cash, dope, guns, and prepared to set the recruits loose on them.

Brian was an interesting guy. He was relentlessly cheerful, quick-witted, and eminently likeable. He showed up wearing coveralls with a medal ribbon pinned to the left breast, and Ray-ban trooper shades. I suppressed a laugh.

"Hey there, Maverick. You feel the need…the need for speed?"

"Ha ha."

"Seriously, where'd you win the medal?"

"Oh, I wasn't in the military. That's my Jubilee Medal."

"Oh man." I rolled my eyes. I spent the next two hours trying to teach deep concealment, while alternately roasting Brian in front of the recruits. What can I say? Jubilee Medals are my trigger. I knew I'd never get one.

"Can anyone tell us why we stopped this vehicle? Bobbi?"

"Because zey vere going vay too fast?"

"Correct!" I yelled at Brian. "Now, Rabbit, step in there, and show us how to swing!"

Class-202 shared my sense of humour. And Brian took it like a trooper. It was probably the last decent laugh I had out there.

The Facilitator's meeting was more heavily attended than I recalled such meetings in the past. Jim and I charged ahead with our concerns. You'd think we'd attacked a member of the family. It was all downhill from there.

Guess who wasn't selected for Use-of-Force Instructor training? Jim, the former Use-of-Force trainer, and me, the guy who'd probably made more arrests than 75% of the faculty combined. Guess who got ratted out for allegedly yelling at his Class-202 recruits? This guy!

Well, I did make them do push-ups. But not that time. Anyway, the bullshit piled up so high and so fast that I soon decided to punch out. I asked if I could get back on at Douglas, and I was told it was affirmative.

When I told the bosses, none of whom would meet with me alone, incidentally, the reaction was shock. Not many people wanted to go back to their home ports, but I was so disgusted with the Rigaud shitshow that I'd gladly forego an extra paycheque a month to be rid of the cliquish old dump.

Au revoir, Rigaud. I was going back to Douglas at the right time anyway. I was going to be there for the Golden Age. I would never have more fun doing my job ever again.

I couldn't wait to get home. But first, I sat in my class, 202, watching them sweat on D-2 day.

And watching every single one of them pass.

TWENTY-EIGHT
THE GOLDEN AGE OF DOUGLAS

I returned to a different world.

The ports had split, meaning you no longer did two weeks here, two weeks there. You chose where you wanted to work. I chose Douglas, which I had always regarded as "the fun place." There was a nice view, the traffic was crazy, there no endless lines of Canadians importing cheap American cars, and I never had to listen to that fucking bus buzzer again.

The new POE was under construction, over the bones of the old Douglas. The temporary port was the sort of place only a government would build with the intent of tearing it down in less than four years. It was lovely, with Immigration on one side, Customs on the other, nice spacious cells (still without toilets though), and only four lanes for regular traffic and one NEXUS.

Fewer lanes meant fewer road times. Fewer road times meant more time to search, which meant more searches, which meant more dope seized.

An influx of keen new officers, foremost among them Trevor and Gorav, meant eager hands looking for dope.

Precious little got away from us in those days. We had the time to search and the motivation to find. We were not tasked with things that did not interest us. So, we began to kick ass.

One dope seizure followed another, in quick succession. You would gear up for a shift, hear about the last major dope seizure, look at the schedule, see you had two road hours in a nine-hour shift, rub your hands with glee, and figure "Let's see what I can get today."

Management briefly abandoned the team concept, then came to their senses, and re-instated it. I wound up working for Kathy, a young-looking woman who nevertheless had been around for thirty years. She was open-minded and friendly to people like me who wanted to kick ass and take names. Kathy liked to talk to people whenever possible but was completely willing to order their asses kicked when necessary. We got along just fine.

Trevor featured in many of the successes of this era. He was a hulking, bald, imposing man physically. Perhaps because of this, he was soft-spoken and deliberate in thought and action. He could afford to be. Within two years of his arrival, he had established himself as a superstar. I worked a couple of major seizures with Trevor in this time. His strengths were twofold; he could question a person relentlessly until they fell apart like an oxtail in the oven. Then, he could, with superlative skill in mechanical arts, disassemble the most elaborate concealments.

Gorav's talents lay in other directions. For starters, I never worked with a better impaired driving investigator. He had an almost supernatural ability to detect drunk drivers, even those whose practised distractions had fooled more seasoned policemen. The local coppers soon came to regard him as the oracle, rather than the other way around. On many other matters, Gorav used his natural abilities as a shit magnet to place himself in the middle of many capers that would otherwise have gone unnoticed.

I prided myself on being a shit magnet. Jim, James, and several of the Bad Boys certainly qualified as well. But Gorav took the all-time trophy.

So good was he at gathering the dark forces of our profession that he began to attract the malevolent hand of death.

People would be talking to Gorav, and would then drop dead, sometimes for no apparent reason. I shit you not, at one point, ambulances would arrive at the POE, and we would call out for him on the radio. "Is this for you?"

"Send it over here."

"DOA?"

"It doesn't look good."

And so, he became known as "The Reaper."

In all seriousness, I'm sure this had some effect on him. It's hard to watch people die in front of you, after all. But humour in law enforcement is merciless. It spared nobody, let alone The Reaper.

One salutary effect of the reduced demands on our manpower: We were now freer than ever before to roam the Park. Though the temporary building had been built with a notable absence of windows on its west side, our camera systems were excellent, and eager young officers with time on their hands were keen to roam, seeing what trouble they could find.

One evening in the summer, Mark, an Immigration type I'd taken a shine to for his snarky humour and willingness to learn, and I were loafing about when we heard a radio call.

"10-33, officers need assistance, we're in a fight, west side of the park!"

We ran across the southbound lanes to find Gorav and another officer in a knock-down fight with a clearly methed-up shitrat in front of a wedding reception.

Yes, there were wedding receptions in the park. 400 plus witnesses for you to ring a suspect's gong in front of. Joy. Mark and I looked at each other and dived in.

The fight ended, briefly, when Trevor showed up and scooped the asshole's legs off the ground. We got him inside, but the little fucker wouldn't quit. I gave him some headshots, and finally we straggled out of the door, covered in indeterminate origin blood and other fluids.

Asshole was a person of interest in two homicides, and the subject of no less than seven deportation orders, who'd last been seen by VPD jumping a fence in East Van. These were the sort of people who strolled through the Park.

Remember that the next time you go down there for a picnic.

In the temporary building days, it seemed as if Douglas' ancient reputation as a nut magnet had multiplied tenfold. Mark and I went to search a pickup truck driven by a California voidoid when I heard a scream from the other side of the truck.

"Shiiiit! There's somebody in here!"

I ran over to the other side and helped Mark yank the trunk monkey out. They literally flew out of their hiding space. Because they were a 99-pound anorexic crazy woman.

She would only give us name, rank, and serial number, you see. She was, after all, a prisoner in an intergalactic war.

I did seriously begin to wonder what planet I was on, after a few years in the temporary building. The constant combat of those years, while exhilarating, left me shell-shocked after every shift, unwilling to talk to anyone who I didn't share a locker room or a bed with. I began to carry extra knives, extra handcuff keys, and start every conversation with "Show me your hands."

There was the Dope Family, whose dad had secreted heroin on himself, then recruited all the kids in his car to hide part of the stash on themselves. There were the two hicks from Oregon who tried to kidnap a fifteen-year old girl and then run from me, only a stalled engine allowing me to catch them. The Hondurans who ran, fought, ran, and fought again.

People crashed and sat still. They crashed, and they ran. I got into so many chases in those days that I limbered up before every shift.

But it was so much fun. We lived on the quivering end of a razor, but we lived there with people we trusted to have our backs. Each shift was a dice roll. What's going to happen today? You didn't know, except that it would be interesting.

I was in the prime of my life. I had the experience to know what I was doing, and I was still energetic enough to have the energy to do it.

What's more, we reaped the rewards of our hard work. Money, dope, and guns flowed down like a waterfall. We were always busy, and if we weren't busting it, we were writing it up.

In those years, I ran into a 28-year LAPD Lieutenant, recently retired, who tried to recruit me.

"Frankly, LT" I said, "I'm having too much fun here."

TWENTY-NINE

TRAITORS

I might have been having a lot of fun at the temporary port. But that didn't change the fact that there were traitors afoot.

Law enforcement isn't just a job; it's a calling. You're supposed to take pride in it and feel loyalty to the community you serve. Now, the CBSA wasn't very good at reinforcing this *esprit de corps,* what with their placemat diplomas, refusal to issue dress uniforms to all, and constant reminders that we weren't trained for this and weren't qualified for that.

But that was never an excuse to break the faith. I've heard all the excuses, and "my bosses are dicks" might excuse laziness or rudeness; it never excused corruption and preying on the innocent. I saw a documentary one time where an American drug cop who went bent explained what tempted him to go to the dark side.

"I was in a room with ten thousand dollars, just sitting there, you can't believe it."

Whatever I was drinking at the time came out of my nose. *Ten thousand dollars?* I'd been in a room with 800,000 dollars, when Dave and Mike from the FRT popped a minivan with cash in every conceivable void. It was stacked along the wall like bricks. If I could stop myself, and they could stop themselves, then anyone could.

Taking a dime was taking a dollar was taking a million. Lying about whether or not a guy had booze on his breath when you pulled him in for an ASD was the same as lying about a confession to murder. Breaking the laws you were sworn to protect was shit behaviour, any way you cut it.

If you couldn't hack these rules, you were in the wrong profession. I wasn't perfect. None of my colleagues were. But most of us tried to remember what the badge signified, and why we'd been given the powers we wielded.

Most of us, that is, except the traitors.

As my career went on, I began to keep count of the people I'd worked with who'd broken the faith. I started being able to count on two hands the number of people who'd proven themselves traitors.

My definition of "traitor" was a pretty constricted one. It didn't include lapses in off-duty judgement, or one punch too many in a use-of-force incident. It didn't include DUIs, although I did notice a few officers who seemed to think this was a recreational sport. It didn't even include people who smoked weed when it was illegal, even though I strongly disapproved.

Traitors were people who used their badge to illegally enrich themselves. They think about it beforehand, and then they decide to betray their colleagues, as well as the people who pay their salaries with their tax dollars. During this time, I crossed paths with three particularly egregious traitors.

The first was good old Al from Team Five. Everybody's pal. Including the organized crime group that got him to run 250 pounds of BC Bud into the US one day, in a minivan.

Whoever Al was working for (he would later say it was a guy named 'Sam' who'd threatened his family) was supremely confident in his ability to elude inspection. The weed was in hockey bags, under a tarpaulin. Al thought he'd breeze through, too, proclaiming his intention to visit the US Port Director.

According to the Americans, he was flagged for a random inspection, but that's what they always say. When he walked into the US Customs office, he coughed it up. Al was nothing if not tight. He had the audacity to call in for family-related leave from a US jail cell. That's how we fired him, by the way. Not the fact that he was a dirty traitor, but the fact that he stole leave from the government. Stealing from the government? Well, you know what the bumper stickers say.

He got off with Club Fed time, a slap on the wrist, considering the betrayal. As for the whole "Sam threatened my family" story, uh…bullshit. Drug traffickers do not threaten unreceptive people who have done nothing to suggest a willingness to compromise their integrity, or an opening for blackmail. They know those people will go to the police.

God knows what else Al did or what he told the enemy. I can't prove anything, so I won't speculate. But I'm guessing Sam got his money's worth.

The next traitor was a man who sold his badge not for money, and not to gangsters. Stickman used his badge to facilitate his own twisted lusts. He used the badge to intimidate naïve young women, usually foreign nationals, into allowing him to perform illegal strip searches.

Stickman was married to Cecilia at the time, a well-respected and liked officer. The way he talked about her, it was as if she was an air-headed housewife, not the tough and competent officer the rest of us knew. He got his nickname from his tall, stoop-shouldered frame. He was serious, bespectacled, and a shade on the arrogant side. He came from a family of cops.

There was no doubt that Stickman was smart, even talented at the job, despite the fact that he was still a rookie. I wound up showing him the ropes. I wasn't as immediately suspicious of him as some.

Ajit coined the name "Stickman."

"He's a fucking nonce, that one. Don't like him."

Jason was not a fan either, although he didn't like a lot of people. But Stickman was impressing some people. He beat me out for a spot on the coveted "Desert Snow" deep search training in Nevada, and he snagged an early spot on firearms training.

But then, Stickman's true nature came to light. I remember that morning clearly. Stickman was coming off of night shift, and I was starting a dayshift. He came up to me and begged me to take an exam off his hands. He never did that. But this morning, he looked like shit, like he was scared, almost.

The day before, Jim had approached me in confidence. "Have you noticed how he's always taking females off to the side, on his own? He's going to get in trouble."

"Yeah, you're right. We'll talk to him next week."

But Stickman knew exactly what he was doing. That day, a woman called Kathy in tears, alleging that her daughter had been strip-searched by Stickman. The RCMP was called in, and Stickman was promptly arrested.

Several other victims were tracked down. Stickman was taking advantage of short-staffed nightshifts to lure women across the street to the park washrooms, where he would get them to disrobe. It was the lowest, creepiest betrayal imaginable.

Stickman destroyed his career, lost his freedom, and his family. Cecilia is now happily remarried, to another officer, and is raising their nearly grown children. Last I heard of Stickman, he was working construction.

A few years later, Pat, one of the most senior officers at Douglas, was working the line when a young woman pulled up. She was meeting an internet boyfriend for the first time.

"What's his name?" Pat asked.

She revealed it was Stickman. The young woman obviously had no clue. "You know," Pat said casually, "It's always a good idea to run a Google search on your dates. You never know. Promise me you'll do that before you meet him, okay?"

"Thanks officer, I will!"

We're watching you, Stickman.

The last major betrayal at Douglas was that of Jas. Jas was a hot shot at deep concealment, an instructor out at the Western Canada Learning Centre, and an idol to young officers. He was cocky and street smart, and when he'd transferred in from Aldergrove, the new Chief had announced, without irony that, "This is the guy who's going to teach you all how to seize dope."

I gritted my teeth. By then, we were in the new Douglas POE, a monster with eight traffic lanes and two NEXUS. Most of us were doing four roadtimes in a 9.5-hour shift. We were now churning out Immigration paperwork. We barely had time to eat lunch, let alone strip down cars anymore for deep concealment.

But Jas was going to teach us something, alright. He was going to teach us just how greedy and amoral a traitor could be.

I didn't like Jas, because I thought he was a dick who'd parlayed a handful of good seizures into a giant reputation and a giant ego to match. Plus, I'd attended a domestic violence call in his primary lane, where he got me to do all the dirty work, while he sat back in his booth and watched. I hated that shit. When I rewind that call in my mind, as I'm marching hubby away in cuffs, there's a motorhome sitting five cars back.

But of course, that's my memory playing tricks. There couldn't have been.

The reason I am sure there was a motorhome there is because that was Jas' MO. He was recruited by a corrupt former RCMP officer to let through motorhomes by prior arrangement. Each motorhome would carry 50-100 kilos of cocaine, plus firearms, for which Jas would be paid 50,000 dollars each run.

That was why he could afford to pay everyone's bar tab. Jas had actually been shuffled to Douglas because he was already under surveillance by a joint RCMP-CBSA taskforce.

When they arrested him, he was extradited to the US, and he got five years in prison.

But the rest of us had to pay. The CBSA was as big a fan of collective punishment as North Korea. That meant we all stopped carrying cell phones, were subject to last-minute changes to roadtimes, and, most damagingly, our access to decent intelligence dried up.

We were no longer trusted. But it was not us who had hired officers without proper background checks. It was not us who had never questioned why officers like Jas were telling new recruits, "You will be approached by organized crime" without asking him to report his contacts, as was mandatory.

That was all on management. But rather than tighten the controls on who they hired, desperate for bodies, they found it easier to view the rest of us with suspicion. The seizures slowed to a trickle, the gradual exodus of bodies became a torrent, and the Golden Age of Douglas came to an end.

THIRTY

STRAP THIS ON

As I awaited my Arming date, set for October 2007, I received a sudden reminder of why we'd been fighting so hard for guns in the first place.

It was early summer, and Lou had taken Woody Allen out to look for guns.

Lou was a big, bald, brown guy with a robust calm, cynical humour, and a genius brain. He was called Lou, and alternately, "Iron Eagle" due to a passing resemblance with Louis Gossett Junior.

Woody Allen was a useless, pint-sized student officer who'd recently been lucky to escape firing after failing to back up a regular officer in a desperate fight with a cokehead. I called him Woody Allen because I thought that's what he looked like, plus I figured he had about as much business in law enforcement as his namesake.

I was casually walking out to secondary when I saw Lou and Woody face-to-face with four large African American males. These men had their hands high in the air. And on one of their hips was a large-frame, semi-auto pistol. The biggest guy, of course.

Speaking of resemblances, the biggest guy looked like Michael Clarke Duncan, from the Green Mile. He was massive. Of course, he was the guy with the gun. Of course.

Well, get them on the ground, I suppose. "Everybody, face down on the ground, now!" As it turned out, they were soldiers, they knew how to follow orders. They were some tense moments as I disarmed the big guy, but my luck held. Walking the big man to cells, I noticed that I could not even come close to getting my hand around the man's biceps.

It was like those old photos of people trying to touch arms around a massive tree trunk.

It all ended well, but the whole thing illustrated what still needed to change in the CBSA. We needed guns to address the tactical deathtraps in a scenario like this. As usual in the past, I believed the suspects complied because they assumed we were armed. What if they didn't? Maybe other people didn't bother themselves with such questions, but I would continue to. Luck was not preparation. The other glaring problem was the presence of unarmed, poorly trained, immature, and often unsuitable student officers on the front line. Their placement at the border was a relic of a much earlier time. Luckily, the government had announced they'd be phased out within two years. But how would the manpower gaps be filled?

Right now, big policy decisions were not my concern. My concern was qualifying to train for arming and passing the course. I had to pass a relatively benign physical, but that wasn't what was really on my mind.

What was on my mind was passing the psych test. Nobody wanted to be exposed as a loon in front of their counterparts. The psych test was double-barreled. First, we completed the Minnesota Multiphasic Personality Inventory. This was a multiple-choice exam which, luckily, had an interpretation guide available on Amazon. I bought one, and it helped me understand certain valuable things. Like, when they ask about flowers, that's code for "gay." And when they ask about "enjoying fire," that's not hot cocoa by the fireplace, that's setting fire to your own house and jerking off till the bucketheads get there. These and other insights allowed me to fool the CBSA into thinking I was sane, despite widely available testimonials to the contrary.

But there was also an interview. I don't remember any of that, except that the interviewer shook so badly that she had to address the issue right off the bat. I couldn't focus on anything else.

It turned out that I needn't have worried. I was certified "sane." Nobody was more surprised than me. Some people had been woefully misjudged by the process.

That couldn't be my concern right now. My concern had to be the course, and my chances of passing. What I was hearing from the first group in was not encouraging. I'd been out in Chilliwack for a few days at the start of the first course for my tactical first aid certification. It was 37C in the sun, and the boys and girls were dissolving in sweat. The pace of training was intense. The course was adapted from the RCMP's recruit firearms training, delivered over six months in Regina, mixed in with other material. This meant it was highly compressed, too much so, as it turned out, in retrospect. Three weeks simply was not enough. Candidates and trainers were working twelve- and fourteen-hour days, and people were starting to drop like flies in the Valley heat.

The agency knew it needed to get as many qualified armed officers on the line before the elimination of the student program made summer training impossible without risking massive lineups. But eventually, the reality would have to be faced: three weeks was not enough.

Towards the end of the July class, I got a text from Julie. She failed. Luckily, she got a spot on the October class with me. I figured we'd be good for each other's nerves. Plus, I could learn a little about what to expect.

October arrived, and we reported for DFA Class 10-2007. Three weeks in RCMP housing, which actually was not as bad as it seemed. They had a hotel company running the whole thing for them. The food was a damn sight better than Rigaud, and the beds were more comfortable.

We became entombed in a single-minded community, isolated from the outside world, unified by the pursuit of a single goal. There were people from Pacific Region, including Kendy, an officer from the Valley who a newly single Julie took an instant shine to. There were officers from the Prairies, Ontario, and Quebec as well.

I took a liking to the Niagara folks. Brett, Jen, and Keely seemed to share a similar mindset with us Douglas types, and they enjoyed the free trip to BC. One of the greatest things about federal law enforcement was the ability to see parts of your own country you never would otherwise. They were especially interested when they saw the Peace Arch Park.

"How do you control this?"

"You don't. Surely you must have similar problems out east?"

"Nope. If you want to get through between the ports out there, you'd better bring a barrel."

The instructors were a generally competent and experienced bunch. They had all passed a gruelling RCMP course in order to teach, and there were some real standouts. The Two Brians were from Pacific Region. Short Brian was a bundle of energy and dad jokes. Tall Brian was a totem of calm and understated humour. Joe was from Calgary, and he was essential in calming me the fuck down when I lost my shit towards the end of the course. Jay was a grumpy guy, having not received good reviews in the first two classes, but gradually he warmed up nicely. I think his problem was he was just too ready to tell Superintendents they couldn't shoot for shit.

However. There was no escaping Kitten. There he was, smarmy smile, lame-ass pronouncements. Always a part of my universe. Luckily, this would be the last time our paths ever crossed.

The days were divided into unarmed combat and shooting relays. The unarmed combat, we were used to, but the shooting took some adaptation. Mostly on account of the characteristics of the pistol the CBSA had chosen.

The Beretta PX-4 was a semi-automatic pistol, like it's competitors, but unlike its nearest competitor, the Smith and Wesson M&P, it was hammer-fired, not striker-fired. This created a problem of anticipation in the shooter, as the trigger pull was tremendously long. The opportunities for jerking the trigger and blowing your shot were frequent and extreme.

Some people liked the gun. While I certainly considered it better than the harsh language that had preceded it, I would've like American steel a little better. My dad had carried a Smith and Wesson Model Ten, I kept a Military and Police 9mm at home, and I knew it was a better combat pistol at the close ranges most gunfights occurred at.

The other problem was the RCMP's continuing emphasis on using a 9 MM pistol for long-range marksmanship, and skewing the course marking towards this skill. Officers were scored 70 out of 250 points for shooting targets out to 25 metres. Instead of learning to kill fast and reload just as fast, we were learning to take our time and slowly recycle our shots. 200 out of 250 was required to pass, and recruits were only allowed to re-shoot a single stage failure. The ranges went from 25 at the outside, to 3 metres at the inside.

I wasn't sure that made any sense, but I wasn't being asked for my opinion. I was being asked to pass. The end of the first week brought Q-1, our first opportunity to qualify. We shot outside, and I had to do a reshoot on Stage 2. My nerves were jangling. Stage 2 was 15 metres, a nightmare combo of fast and far. Twenty seconds for eight shots, four standing, four kneeling.

It might sound like a lot of time, but with a change of position, and the need to sight the targets, it wasn't. The secret was rhythm, and never in ten years did I get it down pat.

But my time had arrived, and at the end of twenty seconds, it looked like I'd made it. I was so fucking relieved.

But then the word came down: "Disqualified. Safety violation. Finger on the trigger."

I lost it. I had a full-on, all-out, temper tantrum. I was mad, mostly because I knew that safety violation was something I'd been doing for two weeks. Somebody should've been watching. And who the fuck takes their finger off the trigger in a goddamned gunfight? Why is that important?

But once Joe got me calmed down, I realized this; the instructors were learning too. And my failures were my failures. I needed to own them.

The next chance I got, I smoked it, scoring 226. I barely made crossed pistols, but I'd done it. The only thing remaining was the scenarios.

Scenarios were mostly fun. For me. I enjoyed situational decision making, and I didn't shy away from it on the line. Those who did, didn't seem to enjoy it so much.

I asked only one thing: let the scenarios be realistic, and let the solutions make sense.

My first scenario was an incredible experience. I kitted up with body armour, facemask, foam baton, inert OC, and simunition pistol with paint-tipped ammunition. Twenty seconds from "scenario on", my traveler had a pistol pointed out the window, trying to end me. I think it was Jay.

The beauty of scenarios was that they fooled you into thinking you really were fighting for your life. The adrenaline and exhaustion afterward were the equal of any dangerous situation I'd ever faced in real life.

Jay's pistol jammed. I could hear him cursing, fighting to clear the jam. I walked around the driver's side and fired two shots into him.

I still had to pass another scenario. This one was very different. The setting, and the suggested response, were bizarre. I was supposed to be working alone in a Customs office, when a deranged man walked in pointing a syringe, and demanding the keys to the POE car.

My natural reaction was to pull my baton. The nut dropped the needle, then went for a stapler off the desk. I stood my ground. When Kitten called the scenario, he had his stern, grownup face on.

Kitten did not approve. For starters, I had my thumbs tucked in my belt "like an old western sheriff." Then, when the loon pulled a stapler, why didn't I pull a gun? Finally, why didn't I defuse the situation by letting him have the car keys?

Wait, what? He's so dangerous I need to pull my gun on him, but I should also give him the keys to a weapon far more dangerous than a fucking desk stapler? I tried to compose myself, but I am sure my anger came through.

"Pardon me. But the only way he could kill me with that stapler was if he took it apart and fed it to me. I'm not pulling my damned gun for that."

A little while later, four RCMP officers at Vancouver Airport tasered Robert Dziekanski during an arrest. He subsequently died. One of their justifications was the fact that he was holding a stapler. I think I won that argument.

They let me do another scenario. I passed.

To this day, it's the hardest thing I've ever had to do. I was proud of it then, and I'm proud of it now. My colleagues and I learned how to confront problems the average person can't possibly imagine. We learned to make the stuff of nightmares manageable.

I returned to my work with a confidence I'd never had before. No more "withdrawal."

THIRTY-ONE

CHICKEN BROTH!

I returned from Arming training with a head full of exciting scenarios and ghoulish training videos detailing the deaths of those unprepared for the last gunfight. I returned with my ears still ringing with the sounds of gunfire, my uniforms still stinking of cordite. I returned to...

Two weeks of Immigration training. Oh, the fun we had. In depth discussions of what keys to press on the 1970s computer system. Permits, documents...hearings!

It was a good thing my gun was still locked up somewhere, or I'd have used it on myself.

To be honest, I was back to reality. All law enforcement work involves a lot of routine. Episodes of *Cops* never centre around routine traffic citations, or dry Break and Enter reports. Sexy stuff, like guns, drugs, fights, and chases, get people to tune in and stay tuned in. I'm as guilty of that as anyone. Most of the stuff I talk about in this book accounts for less that 5% of an officer's career.

But that's the part everyone wants to hear about. The remainder?

Roadtimes without a single interesting person to talk to. Not one. Days where the highlight was an undeclared bottle of liquor, or a harmless lie told about a work permit.

Hardly cops and robbers shit. But honestly, the bulk of our

work. You'll never see that in the recruiting ads, and you'll never see it on an episode of *Border Security*. Why would you?

But the Immigration training foretold a new reality, one I'd feared for a while. Integration had allowed our bosses a way to think of what bosses always wanted to think of: "Doing more with less."

Having never worked the line or having worked it so long ago that taking drunk drivers off the road or seizing dope were not really considerations, our betters viewed any time we were not on the road as down time. I'd been confidently told many times by managers that my night shifts were entirely consumed by watching movies, then having to resist the urge to ask, "You really don't read *anything* that crosses your desk, do you?"

The good times weren't over yet. And it would be a long time before I actually had to learn any of that Immigration knowledge, not a damned bit of which I'd retained, anyway. In those days, under the benevolent neglect of the amiable Old Chief, we were still allowed to act on what I'd come to call Brian's Law, after the veteran who'd coined it.

People are good at what they like. And they like what they're good at.

It was too common-sense a notion for Ottawa to ever be comfortable with. How would you make a graph out of that? But it really meant that, for now, under the leadership of people like Kathy, who preferred effectiveness to the company line, officers could focus on what they knew how to do, and what they took joy in. We still had a few years left to do our jobs.

Before the new sheriff rode into town. In the meantime, officers still found lots of great ways to bore the shit out of each other. Like the old cartoon character said; "We have seen the enemy, and he is us."

One great way of boring the shit out of your fellow officers was Aggie Wanking.

Yes, yes, Food, Plant, and Animal shit was super important, sure. As important as stopping baby rapers and gangsters, okay. If it came to something like Mad Cow Disease, or Avian Flu, I was as ready to buy in as anybody else. But some officers found Aggie referrals so irresistible that they could barely focus on anything else.

Why? I never understood why it was so important to keep Washington State apples out of BC, seeing as how half the apples on sale in our markets had a Washington State seal on them. But, over the years, I developed a theory.

There were officers like James, who knew how to do other things too, and do them well, but also did Aggie. Because, hey, it's what they pay us for.

I suppose I could respect that position, even if I didn't agree with it. But the problem with most Aggie Wanking, in my view, was something very different. A lot of Aggie Wankers did their wanking precisely because it was the easiest way to show they were doing their jobs.

Consider what I'd call, the Hierarchy of Laws (with apologies to Maslow).

Immigration law is calculus level complex. You have to be really smart and David Byrne flippy-floppy in order to get it. I never did.

Criminal Code law required independent thought and flexibility second only to Immigration. That, I could manage, but only just. To some officers, and a shocking number of supervisors, it was too tough.

Customs law was the comfortable province of most. Search people and things, find stuff, seize stuff. Make the right allegation, though, or you're screwed. And make sure you gave them their exemptions. Most of us were hired on our ability to manage this stuff.

Aggie law? Apples: bad. Potatoes: good. There was a binary, 000100100001110 nature to it that appealed to the robotically minded.

This would've been fine if the robots had to clean up their own messes. But they didn't. We had to deal with the pissed-off parents with candy apples, and the Jews who'd been to the kosher butcher and were over their exemption. And we had to act like we cared. It made you want to crawl under your desk and hide.

Special circumstances made the Aggie Wankers even bolder. A short time before I retired, there was a blanket ban on raw poultry and eggs from Washington State due to an outbreak of Avian Flu. The Food, Plant, and Animal geniuses decided we ought to store all the seized poultry and eggs outside, where of course, crows and seagulls landed to have a snack, then flew over Canadian farms and shit on them.

Perhaps, just perhaps, the poultry and eggs would've done less damage in people's kitchens, then their mouths, and then their stomachs. But I don't know anything about that.

Anyway, during this time, the full fury of the Aggie Wankers was felt. Not all of these Wankers were personally motivated.

The agency, by this time, had fallen in love with the tried-and-true technique of management by fear. Managers would cross in the middle of a crisis, expecting to be asked "the question." If they weren't, they'd go after the hapless officer full force, with all the glee you'd expect of the average bully.

So, standing point in the time of Avian Flu was a constant barrage of chicken wings, turkey thighs, and egg whites. But one exchange on the radio was enough to make up for all the aggravation.

Bruce, a former English teacher in China, AKA "Chairman Wow" was a very smart person. Perhaps too smart. See, he'd noticed when supervisors every so often mused aloud, "I wonder how easy it could be to fire you?" So, Bruce took no chances.

When in doubt, he got on the radio. On this particular day, his long-suffering Superintendent, Chris, another transplanted Scotsman, had had enough.

"Uh, is chicken broth allowed, Alpha?"

"What?"

"Chicken broth, is it allowed?"

I heard the world's deepest sigh. "Chicken broth is made from COOKED CHICKENS! IS THIS A BAN ON COOKED CHICKENS, OR RAW CHICKENS? CHICKEN BROTH IS COOKED CHICKEN!"

Even boring shit can be fun, sometimes.

THIRTY-TWO

YOU'RE FIRED

It was around this time that one of my friends, the veteran border pirate Andy, got fired.

Getting fired is difficult, yet not impossible, in the civil service. If you do something sufficiently outrageous, it's certainly possible, like in the cases of the dirty scumbags we discussed earlier.

Andy was not fired for doing anything particularly outrageous. He was fired because he'd built up a cadre of enemies in management. People who said to themselves, "hmm, we'll catch you later."

The Blue Machine does not like being defied. Andy liked to do things his own way, although, truth be told, he was usually focused on the right people. True, his ways were not the ways of most, or even myself, although to be true there was a fair bit of Andy in me. Enough to make me wonder if I was next.

On this occasion, Andy removed a recalcitrant bus driver from his ride. He did not feel like reporting, as he was in a rush. Andy correctly advised him that this did not matter, report you shall, so sayeth the law.

Unfortunately for Andy, one of his passengers was a CBSA manager, and she did not see things his way. The agency bought her line 100%.

Andy never stood a chance. In later years, he landed on his feet quite handsomely, and now runs a successful whale-watching business off the White Rock pier.

For every Andy, there were four or five toxic incompetents whom the agency couldn't, or wouldn't, go after. They preferred to target rebels like Andy, something that made me increasingly nervous as the years went on.

Sometimes, the agency did have to do battle with the truly unsuitable, and the result was rarely pretty. There were so many to choose from.

One of my friends told of a legendary old-timer he worked with at Air Cargo, a man whose prohibited pornography classification scheme was "If it makes me hard, it's prohibited." He liked to break open boxes of chocolates from Belgium for "special targeting," only to realize one time that a particular box contained heroin. How did he write that one up, I wondered?

Closer to home, there was the case of Rejean. Rejean was a former air traffic controller who'd been made redundant by the closure of his airport. There can be few people in history less suited to a uniformed life than Rejean. He did epitomize the old army saying, "ten pounds of shit in a five-pound bag." If asked to refer an exam, he would find some nuns. If told to fill out a referral card for a random project search, he'd scribble "NADA" across it in red pen. Strictly minimal effort.

It was my misfortune, and his, to work night shifts with Rejean. I dragged him into more strip searches than he was, perhaps, prepared for.

But petit larceny and slovenly habits were not enough to support termination. Something more was required.

Jack was one many of us watched, wondering if he was skirting the drain. One day at Pac, I was tasked with backing him up when we took a Pakistani detainee to the washroom. Wet cells, with toilets, were still in the future.

The detainee began to mouth off. Jack just had to reply.

"Listen, you goddamned rug jockey, I know you think your shit doesn't stink, but I'm standing here smelling it, and I can tell you it does. So shut your fucking mouth, wipe your hairy ass, and get back in that goddamned cell before I choke you till your eyes pop out!"

I swallowed hard. How was this gonna go with IAD?

Sure enough, a month later, the dreaded complaint letter came in. I looked it over in terror.

Whatever our opinions about our fellow officers may be, we are not eager to throw them off a cliff to save ourselves, unless of course they are actually outright traitors. But Jack had put me in a tough spot.

Lucky for me, the complainant just went for the full-on, Double Jeopardy lie. Apparently, Lance had pointed a gun at our disgruntled pooper. This was two years before we were armed. No mention of Jim at all. Whew.

The people most of us wanted to be rid of were people like Cindy.

Cindy had been caught with a copy of an intelligence manual, classified "SECRET", in the possession of a shitrat boyfriend. She'd been known to frequent "Angel Acres," a no-class biker hangout on Vancouver Island for scum and the scum who ride behind them.

The agency fired Cindy. But they couldn't do it right, you see. On their first try, they wound up buying her a house. She got her job back, too.

As much as I hated seeing obvious security risks as Cindy keeping their jobs, there was something in her resurrection that appealed to me.

If they went after me, I could beat them. If they bought Cindy a house, they could buy me a yacht.

THIRTY-THREE

CHOIR PRACTICE

Part and parcel of the Golden Age of Douglas was the sense of ownership. We owned the Park. It was <u>our</u> place. We were its kings and queens, not trespassers to be kicked out.

On summer nights, we'd head over to the barbeque pits in the provincial park, as the afternoon shifts let out, and take over. Sometimes, it would even be semi-official, and we'd get inside. Firepits roaring, the ladies would get pretty, and we'd dance and drink until the wee hours.

I think I was the one who christened this "Choir Practice," being a Wambaugh fan. Unlike Wambaugh's Choirboys, we left our guns locked up. We were never seriously challenged, and any Mounties who showed up got a hot dog and an invite to show up later if they could. Border Patrol and CBP guys would drift across, and we'd make it a rager, the fires getting dangerously high, the dances getting dangerously close, the tension of men and women in the prime of their lives doing a dangerous job becoming unwrapped.

American, Canadian, BP, Customs, Mounties, it didn't matter. We were family, and this was as close as we ever came to showing it, outside of a funeral.

These were good times. I slow danced with girls whose names I've conveniently forgotten, but never really will, drank too much and did crazy shit, while somebody, somewhere, mastered the fire and kept the food coming.

Sometimes, Choir Practice was a handful of six packs and a bag of chips. Sometimes it was a big event, with a hundred plus coppers and a standing agreement with the local gendarmes to watch out for us.

It was still the border, so duty intruded occasionally. Me, Mike from the FRT, and my old partner Ross encountered three Hondos sneaking across the line. Of course, we were all drinking, so the cans were kept artfully concealed until the on-duty guys showed up. Then, the party resumed.

I have the sort of hazy memories of those times that I typically reserved for high-school and college debauchery. I loved those people and think that at least some of them loved me. I would look around, and I of course could not conceive that, ten years later, some of them would be gone.

One would not think of such things then. Not in hazy summer air, not with the liquor flowing, the music playing, and soft arms around your waist. Why would you?

We were all in our twenties and thirties then. The idea of death, failure, choosing to move on, that was alien to us all. Some of us had already decided to settle down, but with one foot in the other world, the world of excitement, and people who relied on us, and stories we could only tell each other.

Whether it was a big, or a small affair, the fire would shoot embers into the sky, the war stories would be shouted across the benches until our voices ran hoarse, and we would all somehow make it home.

When I drive past that place, even now, I consider it mine. I earned it. I staked my claim, on those summer nights.

TWENTY-FOUR

CODE FIVE-OH

We had returned from our Arming training with guns on our hips, and a smattering of tactical know-how. But we had returned to a place that was largely unprepared to deal with the new reality.

For starters, most people still did not have the training the eighteen or so of us now had in Pac District. They did not understand lines of fire, cover and concealment, and other concepts that had been pummeled into our heads. This was dangerous, and some of us were awakening to it.

But we'd only been awakened from our slumber relatively recently. So, it took us a few months as a group to take stock. The first thing we needed to get used to was the fact that we were walking around with a gun on our hip.

This is not a natural state of affairs. Even for the son of a cop, like me, the sudden presence of a loaded, deadly weapon on your hip is a bit of a mindblower. If you don't believe me, sign up for the testing and go for it. You'll see I was right.

The ritual, the little steps you go through, every shift, just adds to the feeling of potency. Retrieve gun from locker, holster it. Place magazines, all loaded with seventeen 147-grain hollow point 9 MM rounds into pouches, with one in pocket. Assume position in front of Kevlar panel. Draw, punch out, and load. Rack action and check. Take pocketed mag and place in top pouch.

You are now loaded for duty. If you missed a step, fucked something up, and some bad person pulls a gun and makes a mean face, you will die. And it's all your fault, because you didn't follow training, and you were stupid.

Years later, word got around of some assholes back east who thought the ammo was "too heavy," and went around with eight rounds in their mags instead of seventeen. To think that we fought to get guns for people that stupid really made me want to puke.

Two months after I'd become an armed officer, I was put to the test for the first time.

That day, as very good luck would have it, Dal had, on his own initiative, organized Code Five training for the armed cadre. A "Code Five," in radio parlance, is short for an armed encounter. We practiced rudimentary vehicle takedowns and other scenarios in the Comm Ops lot, thinking our way through the new reality.

A few hours later, I was back at Douglas when I heard a call for backup from the line. I responded cautiously, with Jim and Sarena backing me up. Corey, the primary officer stood in his booth looking at a large African American man in a small beater car.

"He won't respond. He won't even roll down the window or make eye-contact. He's not going anywhere either."

What happened next would likely, in today's climate of hyper-accountability, be condemned as excessive force. But I believe to this day that it was the only solution, and the events of four years later would only reinforce this view. "Get some cover." I told Corey. I drew my pistol and called a Code Five on the radio. Jim and Sarena took up cover positions behind and beside me.

I began to issue short, sharp commands to the driver. Gone was the trance-like visage. It was as if someone had cracked open the ice he was trapped in. Eyes wide, he exited the vehicle, slowly walked towards me, and lay face-down on the ground.

For the first time in my life, I had a loaded gun pointed at another person's head. This is a curious state of affairs for anyone. The importance of all the discipline drummed into us in arming training came home. I was released from the need for conscious thought, and simply acted on reflex. It was only afterward that the reality of it came home.

I can still close my eyes, and see down the barrel of that gun, at another human, lying on the ground.

Once Jim had the guy cuffed, we got him inside and pieced things together.

He was a seemingly sane person with no criminal record. Why the zombie routine?

"I don't have a driver's license."

I'm not sure I bought it. I searched the car and found a large buck knife near the shifter. This reinforced my view that we were being lured in for an ambush, had we decided to try and force our way into the car.

But that was a decision based on instinct. Acceptable then, but in the years to come, as CBSA bureaucrats, people without the instincts of a line officer, insinuated themselves into the review process, it would become less so.

I was sweating the review of my actions a bit. I'd submitted the use-of-force report as required and waited. The next week, Little Brian came out and interviewed me. "Seems fine to me." He smiled.

I knew that the New Chief was not of the same opinion. But nobody was asking him. Still, he had to slip in a lecture about agency values and client service, blah blah blah.

It didn't matter. My actions had passed muster, and my confidence in my ability to make good decisions was reinforced. Some would say a little too much.

After that, a succession of incidents followed. Armed officers were still a rarity, as the limited training spots were taken up by officers from other POEs and divisions. I became a one-man Emergency Response Team, and when I heard my call sign on the radio, I guessed it was for a gun run.

I was working late one night when I got a call from the Silver Fox on primary.

The Silver Fox was such a character I later put him into one of my novels. He was tall, and as the name suggested, silver haired. He was cocky, but not without some cause, as he was quite good at what he did. The old Immigration hand Fred hated his guts. His misadventures with women were legendary.

I came out, cautiously, to find Mark and the Silver Fox with a Bandidos patch holder off his bike, propped against the booth. Lyle stood by the bike. "He's got a gun."

I drew my pistol and said to Lyle, "Move."

Lyle looked at the gun and swallowed. "Okay."

The Bandido was a chapter president from Montana who'd taken a wrong turn with a pistol in his saddlebags. Despite the fact that he was detained as a member of a foreign organized crime group and deported after a hearing, we'd likely done him a favour.

BC was Hells Angels territory. Bandidos were not welcome, especially not flying their colours and packing heat.

The head of the IRB hearing was not in agreement with my actions. But nobody was asking him.

The next summer, it was a time-expired bandit with a couple

of "Armed and Dangerous" flags in the computer system. He looked like he needed a hip replacement, so my backup Terry and I had chat while we considered what to do.

Terry was a veteran who'd worked as a stockbroker in Asia, and who seemed to do the job mostly as a diversion. I suspected he didn't really need the money. In later years we would become friends, but at that time we were still sniffing each other out. Eventually I decided I liked his judgement, and that counted for a lot.

"He's pretty fucking old." I said, as we watched him struggle to get his even more decrepit wife in through the entrance.

"Too old to pull a trigger?" Terry prodded me.

"Yeah." I thought of an incident where US Customs had shot it out in one of their offices with just such a senior delinquent. "Good point."

It went down smoothly. For us. But I did feel badly watching the poor bastard struggle to get on his knees. Past behaviour has present consequences.

For now, if we justified our actions within the confines of law, policy, and training, we were covered. But it was when that began to change that things started to get dangerous again. For now, we knew what we were doing, and people who knew what they were doing reviewed our actions.

But the CBSA's reactions to the actions of the traitors in our ranks was to conclude that more management was what was needed. Clearly, we were the problem, and they were the solution.

The new Director of Pacific Highway District was a take-charge kind of guy who brought a new Chief with him. And the idea of a decision loop they were left out of was completely alien to them.

The fun times would end soon.

THIRTY-FIVE

THE NEW SHERIFF

Be careful what you wish for, as the old adage goes, you just might get it.

The Old Chief was practically invisible, but mostly harmless. He seemed content to let us do our jobs and leave it at that. But with the division of Pac Traffic and Douglas, a position had opened for a New Chief, and so that's what we got.

The New Chief was a physically imposing man with an impressive vocabulary and not a hair out of place. Like most of the men the New Director surrounded himself with, he was a type "A" jock.

He assembled the troops for a "get to know you" session at the Peace Arch park. There we had to sit through a video about some fat buffoon in a Paul Blart scooter harassing skateboarders in Pittsburgh or somewhere. That was supposed to be us.

Okay. So that's the way it's going to be? I felt that familiar vein throbbing in my head, some force in my brain driving me to open my big mouth.

The New Chief had quite a go at us. We'd become badge-happy cowboys who acted like we were policing Los Angeles, not servicing the traveling public. Client service, that was the ticket. We were all going to get an education.

When it came to Q and A time, I had to have a go. This impulse to embarrass powerful people is what has put me where I am today. Exactly nowhere.

"So, Chief, client service is important? So, I guess we should all be more like Al, then?"

"Al?" Someone had to remind him who Al was. "No, of course not!"

"Why not? He was very good at client service. Since you've decided to come in here and tell a room full of people who do good work day in and day out that they're a bunch of mall cops, maybe you can bring him back as a consultant."

The New Chief's eyes narrowed. *Enemy made.*

He went on arming training, scored 250/250, wore the crossed pistols pin around for a few weeks, then put his gear in his locker. But that 250 score convinced him he was an expert on judging our tactical decisions, an unwarranted assumption that would have negative ramifications later.

I felt a growing urge to become a shop steward, just to argue with him. He pronounced that there was no excuse for officers to get complaints. After all, he'd never gotten any as an officer.

I pointed out that, in my experience, the officers who never got complaints never did anything either.

The eyes narrowed again.

The New Chief did enjoy hedging his bets. When the Director became alarmed at all the sketchy people slipping north through the Park, he gathered a group of senior officers and, in confidence, told us that, despite what the agency said, we were free to hunt in the park, provided we could form articulable suspicion for every encounter.

He was good at making a presentation, so I took him at his word.

Problem was, it didn't really mean anything. A few months

later, on the eve of the 2010 Olympics, we spotted a man in camo gear carrying a backpack trying to slip through the woods on the west side of the park. We gave chase, and soon confronted a man who turned on us with an expandable baton. My hand went for my gun. "Drop it!" I shouted.

The man surrendered. We secured the weapon and searched him. He claimed to be a local resident who liked to go for walks in the area and carried the baton for protection from reservation dogs. He had no ID.

"Hey." Trevor looked at the man. "Don't I know you?"

In fact, he did. The man was an RCMP Inspector in charge of an Emergency Response Team. We let him go, but not until I'd let him have a piece of my mind about how close he came to getting lead poisoning.

I told the New Chief, convinced he'd be as concerned as I was with the RCMP playing silly bugger games in our backyard to test our response, which I was almost certain was what had happened. He was more concerned with me going for my gun.

"Can you imagine if you shot at somebody, a Canadian, off the port?"

Yeah, I could imagine. You'd throw me under the bus. I made a mental note: *Support strictly conditional on not making him look bad.*

Don't get me wrong. He was competent enough, and sometimes I even agreed with him. But he didn't fight for us, and when big decisions needed to be made, he insulated himself. At least with the Director, as egotistical as he could be, he'd get in there and take some risks, like commandeering a golf cart to chase down a couple of border jumpers one time. I could respect that.

But the New Chief never wanted to get sticky. Like so many law enforcement managers, he seemed to owe his career to the absence of negatives, instead of the presence of positives.

One last anecdote should serve as a classic example. Not long before I resigned, we received a heads up from intelligence one afternoon. Two males were wanted for murder and car theft in the Seattle area. One of the males was also a Canadian citizen with family in the area, so there was a fairly good chance the two were going to flee north to avoid the needle.

I processed it like everybody else, then went back to work. By then, I was tired of tilting windmills, since it brought me nothing but grief. Besides, the New Chief was in the Superintendent's office with not one, but three Superintendents. Surely, with all that brain power, a plan would arise.

But it did not. I started getting calls at my desk. "Hey, have you heard what the plan is if these guys show?"

"Ask your supervisor. I just work here."

But the calls kept coming, so soon I called the bosses. "Listen, everyone is calling me and wondering what the plan is if these guys show up. People are nervous. Just thought you ought to know, that's all."

Five minutes later, we were summoned to a briefing. Only one person had something more important to do. The New Chief could not be bothered.

Now call me naïve, if you will, but doesn't it make sense that, in an office you ostensibly ran, because your title was "Chief of Operations," that you'd want to be on the tactical planning in case the bad guys showed up? That you wouldn't want to let a notorious hothead like me come up with the plan and run the meeting, which is what happened?

The suspects were caught further down the line, between the ports. But the lasting impression that incident made on me was the importance of avoiding responsibility for the sake of advancing your career. It only contributed to my feeling that the CBSA would not be allowed to consume whatever remained of my life. Not if that was the way things were to be run.

There are many people like the New Chief in the CBSA, and in law enforcement agencies everywhere. Some are worse. At least the New Chief was not tyrannical, or petty and cruel. He was not stupid, or incompetent.

But a place like Douglas required more than just the absence of bad qualities. It required the presence of the good. And as the years went on, I witnessed a slide from the peaks of the Golden Age, into the troughs of the New Mediocrity.

Integration, Luc Portelance, and the Olympics. This would be the trifecta of disaster.

THIRTY-SIX

STUDENTZ

The long-running summer student program, a job-experience/cheap labour initiative, long relied on by the agency to staff during the busy months, was a casualty of the Arming Initiative.

But only at the border. In other locales, like the airport and the cruise ship terminals, summer students, with less than a month of training, make decisions about who will or will not enter Canada unmolested.

If you ever wonder to yourself, "Does my government really care about border security?" then there's your answer right there. They do not.

It's not as if all the students are stupid, or immature, or bent. Hardly. Some were quite brilliant, and a number later went on to become excellent regular officers. But less than a month of training is not considered adequate to do a great many serious jobs unsupervised. Consider the American approach to border security. US recruits must attend a six-month program at the Federal Law Enforcement Training Center before they even allowed in a primary booth. There is no student program.

The US government takes border security seriously. The Canadian government does not.

The final student class at the border was, put simply, a bloody disaster. Dummies, power trippers, and sketch bags abounded. It was a finale many could find appropriate. These people did not belong here.

But it wasn't all like that. The preceding couple of classes had some quality individuals, many of whom went on to be fine regulars. I got to teach officer safety to the newcomers, an eye-opener for many of them. The news that there are people out there who will want to kill you simply because of the uniform you wear is unexpected news in most summer jobs.

Team Five had some great students that first summer I was at the border. Lindsay was a tall, genius-level student from a remote small town. I liked Lindsay. A lot. She now works for the UN with her husband, an ex-British Army engineer who defuses bombs and mines. They are currently in whichever country in the world is in the shittiest situation, since that's where people like that go. If she ever writes a book, now that's what you should read.

France was fun, too, another smart kid and Lindsay's pal. I liked her too.

Some other good ones have stood out throughout the years, many of them becoming regulars, like Gorav, Mike R, Alexandra, Lara, Aman (known for a long time as "Sanjaya" thanks to his hair and Dan's penchant for nicknaming students), and Tina.

Tina is now a Vancouver Police officer like her father before her. She distinguished herself by crawling through broken glass to rescue a fallen comrade during the October 2012 shooting incident.

Roger was an enthusiastic and respectful young man who called us all "sir," until we implored him to stop. He went on to be a dog handler, then a Mountie.

So, to knock all students is not fair. Many did the best with what they were given. The best of the best kept their mouths shut and their eyes and ears open.

But the border is no place for children. And it's no place for the barely trained, either.

THIRTY-SEVEN

DANNY BOY

You know what I hate? What I really hate, worse than American Idol, kale, and Bill Maher?

Cop funerals, and by extension, firefighters' too. Fucking hate them, worse than poison. I won't go anymore, and I made that decision long before I got out.

If you ever read my novels, you will encounter a couple of characters who share my sentiment. These characters, Will Bryant in *Back in Slowly* and Rob Murdoch in *Goodtime Charlie*, express what is pretty much my view. Cop funerals are maudlin, cynical, Celtic celebrations of badge-polishing, excessive drinking, and precision drill, not necessarily in that order. I say that, and I am a product of the culture that created the whole fucking show in the first place.

Most of those in attendance did not know the man or the woman, now forced to lie in a pine box and listen to two hours of bagpipe music. Of those who did, some of them may not have liked the dead hero very much. There is always the cloud of rear-echelon motherfuckers, all at the head of the buffet line, all with the shiniest badges and nicest uniforms.

I know this will offend some. So, understand, this is really only my surface excuse. The real reason is that cop funerals reminded me of my own mortality, my own kids touching my coffin, and my own wife getting a folded-up flag. Who needs that? As for the dead, would they know I didn't go? Would they care?

Another reason I came to hate cop funerals was that my agency made me go to them dressed like a fucking hobo. It was embarrassing, standing next to Mounties in red serge, municipal officers and COs in their dress blues, and me, in unpressable cargo pants and a frayed long sleeve shirt, with a clip-on tie. Yes, I could've joined the Ceremonial Unit and been issued a set of dress blues. But I resisted on principle. I earned that fucking uniform a thousand times over, and I already knew how to march. Not all of my superiors could say that.

No knock against the Ceremonial Unit, to be sure. My friend Theresa has been running the unit for many years now, and with a husband who's worked some of the shittiest maximum-security prisons in Canada, plus what she does, the idea of a line-of-duty death is hardly academic to her. Their presence must provide a comfort to the bereaved. It's just that I can't do it.

My father attended a great many cop funerals in the bloody years of the 1970s and 1980s. Roger Pierlet, gunned down by two punks for sport. Ron McKay, killed by a man with a shotgun my father had seized, and refused to give back to him. Tom Agar, challenged to a quick draw at the front counter. Larry Young, killed by a drug dealer as he led his team in on a raid. Jimmy Ng, hit by a street racer and left to die. That last one was well after he retired. A braver man than I, my father kept going, out of a slavish sense of dedication to his tribe.

But he would never say a damned thing about any of those funerals. He was more willing to talk about autopsies he'd attended, than funerals.

You see, my father and I are, like many Celts, mawkish sentimentalists under the skin. I am reminded of this each time I watch Jules and Gideon Naudet's masterful documentary 9/11. At the end, after the horrible scene where one of the brothers stumbles through the ruins of the South Tower looking for the other, to the tune of hundreds of personal alarms screeching, the credits play over 343 pictures of dead firefighters.

I cry every time, and I am a little soft right now just thinking about it. "Danny Boy" plays, of course. I walk away when I hear that song.

I did make it to three funerals. The first was Greg Brady's.

Greg started as a student, nicknamed "Beav" for the gap in his teeth. I used to work graveyards with him. One day, he was coming home from work, when for whatever reason, he turned in front of a dump truck.

It was my first experience with such a spectacle. There must've been a thousand officers and other well wishers there. I got out as soon as I could.

The next was Adrian Oliver. He was a Surrey RCMP member, whose twin brother was also a member. This funeral was huge, with something like 5000 officers and others in attendance at an arena in Langley. The circumstances of his death were eerily similar to Greg's, except he was on night shift, turning in front of a truck. How many times had we all almost done the same thing?

The video presentation got to me. Him and his brother, particularly. I ran from that one, too.

But it was Louis Beglaw's funeral that made me say, no more. Lou was a dog handler with West Van PD, who I'd worked with at Pac Highway years before. His wife, Sarah, was a CBSA officer. Lou had suffered a heart attack in the gym at his office. When she brought their two small children up to the coffin to say goodbye, it was enough for me. I really ran from that one, after turning to Lyle and saying, "I am fucking out", determined that I would never do it again.

Luckily, I haven't had to choose lately. But if you're reading this, know this: if you die, I am not coming to your fucking funeral.

No offence.

THIRTY-EIGHT

CELEBRITY JEOPARDY

Celebrities. Some people are quite thrilled to meet them. Me? Meh, I could care less. So, I suppose this particular facet of the job was wasted on me.

Celebrities must cross borders, following the same rules as the rest of us, a reality which irks some of them beyond belief. Some travel on private jets to assure minimal hassle as a result. Others fly commercially, assuming nondescript looks to avoid detection, or being so normal looking anyway as to escape attention. Some who did fly commercial seemed to enjoy the attention anyway.

At the border, we often dealt with celebrities coming down to renew their work permits, or driving up from Seattle, or just living their day-to-day lives.

Vancouver is also known as "Hollywood North," a city with a wide range of neighbourhoods and landscapes that can double for practically anywhere. It also offers American producers a favourable exchange rate, advanced production facilities, and talented crew and supporting actors. In recent years, many Hollywood types have acquired property in the Gulf Islands, or in Whistler.

So, I crossed paths with quite a few celebrities. Most, even those with difficult reputations, tended to be well-behaved. Why? I think that, simply put, they knew we had to deal with them, and they had to deal with us. We weren't following them and their kids around with a telephoto lens. I tried to always keep this in mind while dealing with celebrities. Treat them as ordinary people, no better, no worse. If you liked their work, mention it casually. Everyone likes to be liked.

I was standing point in the airport one day when a celebrity with a reputation for punching photographers walked up to me. He handed in his declaration card with a smile. I was stupidly proud of myself for getting that close to him without sustaining an uppercut to the jaw.

Another time, I was clearing a flight from LA when I had to call a very tall passenger up several times. He was engrossed in conversation with his fellow passengers, who seemed quite enamoured of him. I recognized him as having formerly been married to a very tall actress who once drove off a cliff in a movie, and as having spent a fair bit of his career running from CGI dinosaurs. He was a very nice man, and after answering my questions, he proceeded to extract a promise from me that I would see his next movie.

I lied, of course, but he was a nice guy. I didn't have the heart to let him down. I don't think very many people saw that movie.

There was really only one time I thought I had a fighting chance at picking up a celebrity. She was very short, with big brown eyes and a sultry, quiet voice. There was some sort of chemistry there, or at least I figured as much. This actress had become famous playing a character who lived with her very strange family in a haunted house and was named after a day of the week.

No, I didn't ask her out. She was famous, and I was on duty. But I bet I could've pulled it off. I swear, there was something...

Another very nice actor I ran into at the border had starred in one of my favourite war movies, helmed by a legendary director. He'd spent the first half of the movie being yelled at by a real-life drill instructor, and ended the movie singing the theme from a 1950s TV show. I couldn't resist pulling some production stories out of him, and he was happy to tell them.

So, most celebrities behaved themselves, and were fun to meet. But others behaved with varying degrees of delinquency.

Bands could be trouble. They tended to travel with entourages of crew and hangers-on, and this almost always resulted in somebody having Immigration problems. Often, the people left behind at the border could be done without, but sometimes, we closed the show.

When this happened, often because the lead guitarist was a rapist, or the drummer got caught with a kilo of blow, the bands would inevitably lie through their teeth about it. "We got hassled for no reason at the border!" they would whine to the media and their fans.

Rappers were the absolute fucking worst. One famous, very tall and very skinny rapper, who exists in a perpetual cloud of dope smoke, was always a chore to deal with. He never seemed to learn that, whenever he brought dope, or large amounts of undeclared cash, he would lose it.

Of course, he always made his show, because he was a big deal. There was a certain amount of economic discrimination in deciding who got a Temporary Resident Permit to cancel out their bad behaviour. If you were another notorious rapper, named after an amount of currency, you would get a permit, because you could fill Rogers Arena. Regardless of how many times you'd been shot.

But if you were in an indie band, and you had a burglary rap, you were fucked. You were probably only going to be playing in front of a hundred people anyways.

My favourite band was due to perform at the Commodore one night, and I had tickets. I learned though that the lead female vocalist had a meltdown at the border and wasn't going to play. Her boyfriend was an American who was criminally inadmissible, and when she found out that was an issue, she decided to try and throw her weight around.

Unfortunately, she was dealing with my friend Graydon. Graydon was a veteran with a talent for staying calm and shooting back when besieged by bullshit. He let her have it, in no uncertain terms. Sit down/shut up.

I went to the concert anyway, and it was the best time I'd ever seen them live. Maybe she was overrated.

Andy was searching an old country music star's bus one time, when the star asked him, "Whatcha all looking for, anyway?"

"Contraband."

"Why, we's a country band."

Athletes could pose some special challenges. Many of my fellow officers were much more enthusiastic about dealing with them than I was. Personally, I hadn't given a shit about sports since the Canucks blew the '94 Cup run.

Speaking of the Canucks, they were coming off a plane from Boston when their star performer at the time, a hulk who later delivered a devasting and dirty hit on a Colorado Avalanche, gave me a declaration card with his name not filled in. Bit of a basic oversight there, sport. I handed it back to him and told him to go back to the table and fill out completely. He took the card in a huff but did as he was told. All the while his teammates chanted the letters of his name as he struggled to fill it out.

I was glad I could give them some entertainment.

Some celebrities got into worse trouble. I saw a couple in airport secondary, handcuffed, while drug paraphernalia and little envelopes with white crystals were pulled out of their bags. Who this would be was never surprising. Those celebrities who you looked at pictures of and figured "They must be on drugs."

Yes, you're right. They are.

THIRTY-NINE

THE BATTLE OF THE PEACE ARCH

The year before the 2010 Olympics was the debut of the massive new Douglas Port.

It was a classic civil service triumph of form over function. "Ooh, it looks like an overturned boat!" "Ooh there's so many windows!" "Ooh it has such a nice overhanging roof!" The travelers couldn't stop gushing.

Yes, yes, great. So many windows, yet none of them looking west, where so many of the illegal crossers were. Overhanging roofs that didn't keep you dry all the way in the front doors, and in the winter, dropped dangerous shards of ice on your head. Long counters whose only exits to the lobby were 30 metres apart, meaning, if you needed to help someone in trouble, you needed to vault the counter at one very particular point.

Now, we'd been asked for our input. But little or none of that input had been used. I would recall, bitterly, a couple of years later the laughter that had greeted my suggestion of ballistic glass in the primary booths.

But it wasn't all bad. We had four wet cells. A proper change room, although when we opened, one of the toilet stalls hadn't yet had its walls installed. That didn't stop one of the IT guys from going in on a bomb run.

Mark walked in, mid-poop. "Er. Ah, hello."

"Ahem. Hello."

The facility was certainly better than the decrepit old dump it had been intended to replace. But its biggest problem was one of emphasis. The new facility had eight traffic lanes, and two NEXUS lanes. There were 25 parking spots in secondary.

Anyone experienced in border operations could take one look at this and predict what a mess it would be on a Saturday night. Had they not spoken to anyone? Or had they all just pretended it was fine? It was the preferred way to go in the CBSA.

Our first summer in the new building was marked by an outflow of experienced hands to the ever-expanding Inland Enforcement operation, as Canada's government finally got around to deporting some of the 50,000 people it had ordered to get out. New recruits took their places, but new recruits took time to train.

We also had to deal with park issues more often. The new building was square in the middle of it, whereas the old facility had been on its edge. That presented some problems.

Vancouver had a growing population of Afghan refugees. They enjoyed recreating in the Peace Arch Park, which was a problem for us, because many of them seemed not to understand that the "Park" was also a "Border." No, kids, you can't fly your kites across seven lanes of traffic.

Part of living in an immigrant society is mastering the difficult art of cross-cultural communication. One Sunday afternoon would make that challenge abundantly clear.

It would also highlight the tensions between the bosses and the rank-and-file, and the agency's policies versus the real requirements of public order and safety.

That day, the Afghans had their picnic. Fifty or so people were there. And then, someone kicked a soccer ball off of grandma's head.

I was standing out in secondary with an RCMP Freeway member and some other officers when Sina casually noticed, "Hey, is that a fight over there?"

"Holy shit!" The RCMP officer was booting it for the wide-open field on the west side of the park. We followed. Ahead of us, at least twenty-five people, surrounded by at least as many spectators, were engaged in a furious brawl that seemed to have spontaneously combusted.

I was calling in a 10-33 before we even got there. The crowd looked nasty as fuck; we were way outnumbered. In seconds we had reached the edge of the furball. I drew my baton and looked around. "Get your sticks out!" I yelled to the new guys.

Behind us, the spectators were becoming more active, turning their anger on us, screaming and gesticulating. *Time to go on the offensive.* I waded into the brawl, my baton in cross-check mode, pushing back the crowd. "Back! Get the fuck back!" I found one heavyset Afghan on top of another, pummeling him. Both men were covered in blood. I reached in, grabbed his right arm mid swing, planted an arm bar, and levered the man on top off of his prey.

The crowd parted. Wielding a 300-pound man covered in blood can have that effect. I kicked his feet out from under him and planted him to the ground.

But as I was trying to get the cuffs on him, the crowd started surrounding us. On the radio, my requests for backup were being countermanded by the Superintendents. I got on the air again. "Get me some backup over here now! All available units! Now!" I tried to form the people I had into some sort of skirmish line. Women from the crowd were getting bolder, led by one shrieking harridan in particular. *I must be kneeling on her husband.*

"Keep this bitch off me while I cuff him! Get back!" I waved my baton at the crowd while a couple of officers got between me and the cheerleading squad. Sweat was pouring down my face as I cuffed the big man and struggled to get him up. When I stood, I saw a tremendous sight.

It was a peculiarity of the schedule we had back then that on Sundays, we had three teams on duty instead of one. We also had an almost full complement of staff. Lots of officers had heard our calls.

Now, 25 officers formed a solid blue line and began to advance like a Roman Legion into the crowd. I passed off my prisoner to a couple of the new arrivals and scanned the still going brawl. "Form a line. Push 'em back!" We began to press the hardcore brawlers. Other officers picked out a couple of hard swingers and knocked them to the ground. We rampaged over the centre of the fight like a multi-headed steamroller, swinging batons and pushing. "Disperse! Disperse now or you will be arrested! Disperse!" I screamed until I was hoarse.

Then, an RCMP car mounted the shoulder behind us Code 3, and Pete, the Freeway Corporal raced to assist us. I later found out he'd done 140 km/h from the Alex Fraser Bridge. I scanned the crowd for his man and found him on the far west edge of the fight, squared off with a giant freak in a mohawk, whose face was already bloody. I broke out my OC spray, pointed my can at the screaming freak, and prepared to let him have it.

Now, I really have no idea how a giant Caucasian mutant with a mohawk ends up at an Afghan picnic, but I'm sure it would've been an interesting story if I'd ever heard it. But the sight of two cops instead of one about to beat the shit out of him made this Fauxhawk take to his heels.

As suddenly as it had started, the battle was over. We packed our cells full, summoned ambulances, and dispersed the rest of the picnickers. Meanwhile, the single member Surrey RCMP had casually dispatched watched with one of our Superintendents.

The next day, the Surrey RCMP spokesman claimed credit for breaking up the riot in the local power. That didn't go over well with our Director.

While at first, it seemed I would get in some shit for countermanding orders, the gratitude of the Freeway RCMP members saved my ass. I got away with my little Admiral Nelson act, this time at least.

As for the Afghans, they got patched up and sent home.

"Trying to get a straight story out of this bunch," One RCMP member told me, "Is like trying to get a whisky rocks in Riyadh."

FORTY
LUNATICS

With all the changes at the border, here's one thing that was always the same, from day one: Borders are a magnet for lunatics, the lost, and the seriously shitfaced.

When I started writing this book, I thought I'd run out of room with just my personal recollections. Then other people started sharing theirs. From this, I have come to a conclusion: Five years at Pacific Highway ought to count towards two years of a psychology degree.

People who show up at the border often have classical DSM-IV symptoms. They are disoriented. They are delusional. They are panicked. They engage in risky behaviour. Ask any officer who has spent six or more months at a border crossing, and they'll tell you: there isn't enough Prozac in the world for these people.

Why would that be? I mean, it's just a line drawn across a map, for Christ's sake.

I have a few ideas, actually. People with mental illness often develop fixations. Obsessions with utopias, where they can flee from the KBG/CIA/Holy Roman Church. Sometimes, some very unhealthy obsessions with law enforcement.

Anyone who puts on a uniform understands this one. The sad and the lost are drawn immediately to you. Put your office at the end of a straight shot all the way from Tijuana, and there's no way they can miss you.

Crazy people are always looking for an escape. I remember chasing a naked woman through the International Departures security checkpoint when I worked at the airport. I have no idea how she got to the airport, but there she was, starkers but for a pair of granny panties and a copious supply of body hair. When I caught up to her, she only had one question for me:

"Am I in Australia?"

"Um...yes. Mate."

Pacific Highway may be a little jog off the straight shot from Tijuana, but it does have something Douglas doesn't: The Buses. Buses are the classic low-income transportation, getting a poor person from Seattle to Vancouver for under a hundred bucks.

So, when that buzzer went off, you could be in for interesting times. I remember clearing a Seattle Quick Shuttle. The first person off the bus was a giant Nordic type wearing a Tyvek suit. He had written the word "Marijuana" on every limb in green pen.

Feeling insightful, I decided to forego the usual foreplay. "Say there, you got any marihuana?"

The Cannabis Viking proceeded to remove fistfuls of bud from every pocket, setting it on my desk. "It's okay, officer. I have a note." He put a note filled out in green pen, by Doctor Him, on the desk. Medical marihuana it is.

"Okay, then."

I sometimes felt bad about this next one, but it was so funny I could never completely be ashamed of it. In the mid 2000s, internet dating was still a novelty. But so often, the thrilling life partner prospect showed up on the Quick Shuttle.

This life partner prospect was greeted by her prospective fiancée and his mother. He brought an embarrassingly large bouquet. They waited, expectantly, on the other side of a glass wall separating the Bus Immigration area and the main office.

Of course, Team Five was gathered, watching, already snickering. We already knew that the Bus Bride had an impressive felony record, and flowers or not there was no damned way she was coming in.

The final separation was heartbreaking. Faces pressed against the glass, the lovers parted, never to meet. Of course, we were all hiding behind the counter, trying to keep from peeing ourselves.

Yes, we were dicks. But if you've done as much amateur psychology as us, you need to blow off some steam.

Not all bus loonies were so hilariously harmless. There was the tiny Asian lady with the shaved head who decided she needed to escape being raped all the time (male officers beware; this is a frequent motif) by making a refugee claim in the US. When this was refused, she returned and put a brick through the cashier office window, narrowly missing one of our people.

One American, displeased at being sent back on a late bus, declared he would come back and chop Lyle and Christian into tiny pieces with an axe. Since this was before the days of firearms, when our answer would be, "Sure, bring that to a gunfight, asshole," this triggered a whole night of police babysitting.

The lost were another story. Some were led astray simply by low IQs and a shitty knowledge of geography. The whole "Vancouver Washington/Vancouver BC" thing accounted for many casualties. Like the US Army wife who decided to go for a drive with one of her husband's war trophies, an Iraqi grenade in her glove box. Jim got to deal with her, and the Bomb Squad, while I got to deal with the NEXUS members who thought their fifty bucks every five years included shrapnel protection.

GPS got lots of people, more as the years went on. Early GPS units would predict the shortest route no matter what, even if it did lead you across a border. The Mexican population of Northwest Washington was reduced by a significant percentage as a result. States love to indulge in "sanctuary" policies, but federal governments have no such leeway. Legal is legal, illegal is illegal. We would feel sorry for these poor, often hardworking people, but since, so often their misfortune was accompanied by a DUI, something they could prevent if they wanted to, this pity was limited.

The Fabulous Reverso Brothers were a classic example of the Wrong Way Jose. We were hanging out in Douglas when Jason peered at the monitor.

"Hey. Those fuckers are backing up down the freeway."

"Fuck, they are!" A bunch of us raced out of the office and charged down the hill. On the way, I got a radio call.

"They just did a driver swap."

Great. Two for the price of one. When we arrived, their Jeep was sitting on a massive boulder, rocking back and forth, wheels still turning. When I arrested the driver, a noisemaker was sticking out of his breast pocket.

"Ohh mang, my girlfriend, she leave me. I'm so sad, Mr Police, so sad. My cousin, he a policeman in California. My girlfriend, she leave me!"

Jesus, three hours of this. At least his cousin the cop in Cali made him come back and plead guilty.

But the all-time, champion "Holy shit, were you high" driver was the man who flew through the Duty Free. It was almost midnight when we heard a tremendous, nuclear smash. When I got there, I found a massive hole in the Duty-Free window. A car was neatly deposited in the whisky aisle. Along its probable route, saplings were sliced in half. After Cory, Jessie and I cleared the store, fearful of smash-and-grab robbers, I stepped out of the store and looked around.

In the middle of the highway, an impeccably dressed East Indian man stood, as if looking around in his living room for a lost TV remote. I walked over to him.

"Hiya. I'm Officer Patterson."

"Hello. Have you seen my watch?" He stumbled into me.

"No, but I have found your bracelets." I took my handcuffs out. "You're under arrest."

FORTY-ONE

THE TRIFECTA OF DISASTER

The much anticipated 2010 Vancouver/Whistler Olympics arrived with a giant plop.

The Olympics were a hit everywhere else, but someone in Ottawa had overestimated the financial means of the average land border traveler. Since event tickets, even for the lamest sports, were going for hundreds of dollars a pop, most middle-class people couldn't afford them. The stands were filled with the rich, and the comped.

This meant that the 20-odd officers brought in for the event from all over Canada had little to do besides man almost-deserted booths, and bitch about their own managers. Since most of them were not Immigration-trained, they couldn't help out with what had rapidly become our singular obsession.

It was always eye-opening to listen to stories about how the CBSA did business across a vast country. Some managers seemed to be refreshingly common-sense, like the one Chief who analyzed what a sensible threshold for duty and tax would be at his port, and told his troops, "That's what I want, do that." We, on the other hand, were always left to guess.

Mostly, though, we heard horror stories of the sort that actually made us want to hug some of the people we worked for. Apparently, it was routine for a lot of managers back east to call "BSOs" "Bozos." Ha ha. You didn't talk to your boss unless you had a shop steward with you, period.

Had it not been for the ridiculous BC cost of living, I think a lot of them might have put in for transfers. But their temporary presence had a sinister effect I'd anticipated long before the Games.

Travelers don't like lineups. Nobody does. And since most travelers (and a fair number of managers) think we are jerking off when we're not on the road, they want to see open traffic lanes, used or not, as the visible evidence of what they're paying their taxes for.

We got them hooked on not having to wait. And when the transplants went home, the expectation remained. See, just as travelers love seeing empty traffic lanes, bosses love reading compliments, like "No waits, how wonderful!"

So, no matter how thin we were on the ground, we were expected to keep the maximum number of lanes open. Where only a few years ago it was no big deal to close a lane if we had something big going on, now it took a lot of convincing.

Senior people like me, people known to be prickly, had no problems fighting for what we thought was important. But the problem was that there had been a drain on the senior staff, and now there weren't many of us left. Junior officers caved under the pressure to cater to the traffic, and good enforcement was kicked up the road.

Everyone knew it was happening, but nobody would admit it. This was the first element of The Trifecta of Disaster.

The second was closely related: Integration. It seemed logical to train everyone to do everything, and I agreed, up to a point. But soon, it was not unusual to see old Customs hands puzzling over a work permit application, while unsupervised rookies botched a drug exam a few metres away. Nobody seemed to care that people who were very good at some things that very desperately needed to be done, were not being allowed to do them.

Soon, Douglas became a permit factory. Citizenship and Immigration was scaling back it's domestic services, prompting immigration consultants to tell their clients to flagpole in order to skip the lineup. "Flagpoling" refers to visiting the border to obtain services only available to people entering from outside Canada, but in reality, simply visiting US Customs, turning around, and coming back. It was an egregious abuse of what a POE was supposed to be there for, but soon, it was our primary preoccupation.

We catered to this bullshit 24/7. Rather than display some testicular fortitude and at least say "business hours only," we pumped out permits at 0200 if requested, while our colleagues arrested drunks and psychos in the same office. We made consultants rich, and the taxpayers poor. It was one of the stupidest things I've ever seen a bureaucracy do, and it took a worldwide pandemic to end it, at least temporarily.

Canada seems to be hooked on a perennial influx of people to solve any and all of its problems. We would rather import Tim Hortons servers from the Philippines than pay our own teenagers and retirees a few extra bucks to do the same job. We treat our native-born population the way we treat old electronics; don't fix it, toss it, and shop around for something better.

So many of the permits were such obvious, cynical shit. "Skilled worker" and "sandwich maker" came to mean the same thing. Bogus diploma mills pumped out degrees to rich wastrels interested only in the post-graduate work permits, which then would lead to permanent residence. The provinces vouched for much of this garbage as "essential."

Driving down the road to Douglas some mornings, one could catch a hydrogen sulfide smell in the air. That was actually the Cherry Point Refinery south of the line burning off waste gas, but to me, it increasingly smelled like the stink of corruption.

We were peace officers, involved in perpetrating a fraud. This was the second element of The Trifecta of Disaster.

The last element was our new President. I always found this terminology strange. "President," instead of "Commissioner," sounded too corporate to my ears for a law enforcement agency.

But hearing of the background of Luc Portelance, the former Mountie turned CSIS official, gave a lot of us hope that the shaky reign of the Weatherman Jolicoeur was dead and buried forever. After all, he had come from a law enforcement and national security background, so he might see things our way, right?

How wrong that assumption turned out to be. Portelance seemed to view us as poorly trained dilettantes, compared to his elite background, and fretted at any expansion of our duties. He once lectured Jessie at length during a visit to the POE about how we weren't trained well enough to walk across the street and say "come here" to somebody crossing the border.

And he was a fan of draconian discipline, as we would soon find out. Like the New Chief, he was another believer in the "border cowboy" problem, seeing Paul Blarts under the bedsheets. Suddenly, leaving an empty gun locker unlocked in a locked gun room could get you a suspension.

Apart from what he did, there was just what he didn't do. He didn't seem to have anything nice to say about us, or what we did. We were more of a problem, than a solution.

I don't know why I expected anything different from the CBSA. They never did anything but disappoint us. Portelance's disheartening leadership was the final element of The Trifecta of Disaster, ending the brief, hopeful period, when it seemed that the agency would become a real law enforcement concern. Instead, it was back on the short bus for the Bozos.

The pilot RCMP-CBSA border patrol project was relegated to Western Quebec, where it died the expected quiet death. The

A LIFE ON THE LINE

fantastically popular *Border Security* TV show would eventually have its cameras unplugged by Ottawa after Civil Liberties activists objected to illegal workers being caught on camera working illegally. A trained cadre of uniformed spokespeople were kept in the closet, and we returned to public relations by silence.

Increasingly, my motto became "Ah, fuck it." I had bigger things going on in my personal life, anyway. In 2008, Diana and I had gotten married. In 2010, we welcomed our first child.

Diana had felt more comfortable giving birth in Brazil, so I took a few months of parental leave to be there. It was hard to think of coming back at first. My wife would often ask me, after I would come home from work and vent, "Why do you put up with these bullshits?"

Sitting in the sun in Sao Paulo with a caipirinha, I would wonder exactly that. *Why do I put up with these bullshits?*

But then I started watching old *Cops* reruns, and I got to missing it. So, I came back.

But the seed was already planted in my mind. *I don't need this shit.* And soon, the agency would water the seed.

FORTY-TWO

ASSHOLES

I shall call this chapter "Assholes," because that is exactly what it is about. Not management assholes, or shithead lawyers, or pesky immigration consultants with dubious clients.

No, this is about people who have nothing better to do than pick fights with us when they choose of their own volition to cross the border. While some people enjoy drinking and sex, these people enjoy fighting and complaining.

Their complaints are almost always entirely worthless, which is why I always argue with managers who insist that one complaint is one too many. These people complain as a way of life. And, if you look into their backgrounds even just a little, you quickly find out that it's not just us; no, they have a beef with literally anyone who crosses their path and does not immediately say "yes, sir."

After a few years of dealing with assholes, I could sense when one of them was probing me for weakness. Not all of them pulled up screaming and shouting, like in Rigaud. I was on primary one night when a middle-aged white man (the typical asshole demographic) pulled up. He gave my gun a pointed glance.

"Is this a new thing for you guys, or is that just something you decided to do on your own?"

Deflating his "I'm a hero" bubble, I briefed him on the new Arming initiative and invited him to make his feelings known.

"Hmm. Okay." As in, "I'll let it go this time."

That guy was an amateur, for a professional, let me introduce you to BA. BA wasn't looking too good the last time I saw him, so perhaps I am speaking ill of the dead. No apologies, since this one miserable bastard probably contributed to the hypertension of dozens of officers. He was that bad.

I could've nicknamed him "Mr Root Canal," since talking to him was that painful. He is the only man I know who was prohibited from complaining. Period. On order of Headquarters, since he had abused the privilege so often. He was once famous for leaving the primary line, after ensuring a peptic ulcer for the officer therein, and driving straight to secondary, referred or not, where the Old Old Chief would be waiting for him.

Tina maintained that she got along with him fine. "We talk about potatoes."

Sounded about his mental equivalency. Anyway, I had luckily avoided BA for years until one day at Douglas. FRT was running a project on vehicles I'd released, trying to make me look bad, as usual. A crapped-out minivan with a smug-looking driver, a snarly female, and two miserable-looking kids pulled up. Nobody had any ID out.

"Sir, may I see everyone's proof of citizenship."

And, so, it began. Like that scene in Borat, when he walks into a cheese shop, and asks what everything is?

"What is that?"

"Cheese?"

"What is this?"

"Also cheese."

"I'm sorry sir, a UK birth certificate on its own is insufficient.

Do you have any proof of Canadian citizenship, or residency, and some photo ID? And I'm afraid I'll need that for all occupants of the vehicle."

And so it went, for a good ten minutes. The angrier he got, the sweeter and more patient I got. I knew who I was dealing with, and I was damn sure going to give not an inch. Eventually, I handed back the 46-some-odd pieces of ID for four people and concluded the interview. "Thanks so much for your time."

"I shall complain about you. What is your name and badge number?"

"Oh, really? Complain about what? See, I heard you weren't allowed to complain anymore. Better not pull over."

"I shall complain. I shall complain to the Prime Minister, Paul Martin."

"Yes, I know his name too. Great. You do that, and I'll write a response. Have a super day."

He pulled out of my line, and right over to poor Nick from the FRT. When I got out of my booth ½ hour later, he was still there. The answer to "Don't these people have anything better to do?" is "No, no they don't."

Several years later, I ran into a much older, and sicker looking BA. I was doing random searches of NEXUS members, and he was sent over to me. "Do you know who I am?" Clearly, he still believed he was Lord Voldemort.

"Yes. Stand over there please."

"Do you know I got your Chief fired?"

"No, you didn't. I went to his retirement dinner."

"Well, when this is over, I should like to talk to your Superintendent."

I looked over to where Marcus, newly transplanted from the airport, and already acting Superintendent, was supervising things. Marcus was a good guy. But hey, part of being a Superintendent was learning how to deal with people like BA, right?

I laughed an evil laugh to myself. "Most certainly, sir."

When I walked away a half-hour later, BA was still chewing Marcus' ear off. When he finally caught up with me in the locker room, Marcus was succinct.

"I'll fucking get you for that."

"Tee hee."

There is a legendary asshole at Pac Highway. Let's call him "Dave Stanford", because he's also named after a university. When Dave shows up, apparently there's a special code to accommodate his adult diaper theatrics.

I've never dealt with him myself, but the thought of delivering a straight palm-heel strike to his jugular was always tempting. He'll push the wrong button, with the wrong person, someday.

Every officer has their "my last day" fantasy, that special asshole they want to run into on their last day and deliver a monumental beat down to.

Meh, I used to. But as the years went on, I replaced my last day fantasies with the sincere wish that nothing at all would happen. My big fantasy? Filling out some forms, turning in my gun and my badge, and walking out the fucking doors. Ahh.

Alas, two weeks from retirement, another legendary asshole caught up with me. I shall call him "Dudley Do Wrong," because he was an ex-Mountie, and possibly the largest prolapsed asshole I have ever encountered on this earth. I mean, every time anyone who is even slightly less of an asshole dies, we should mourn them, for there is more oxygen for this fuckstick.

There were lots of nasty rumours swirling around about him, nasty, nasty ones, concerning his hasty departure from the force and other matters more serious. But I shall not repeat them, for I hear he wants to sue me, and there is no way this living, breathing defecate shall ever touch a cent of my children's inheritance.

Trevor had some nice run ins with him, seizing a sports car and a computer from him in a couple of separate incidents. But Trevor has the patience of Jesus Christ, and he apparently stage-managed the adult toddler show that is Dudley.

He would cross, I would recognize him, and things would be fine. If I needed to refer him, I did. If I didn't, I let him go. Yes, he was smug, somewhat douchey, but I let that slide. Who needs it? I was beginning to think his rep was maybe a tad pumped-up.

Meanwhile, over at Pac Highway, Dudley went too far with the Big Fish. The Big Fish is a very large man, competent in the art of Fuck-Yu. Dudley went for a ride into a computer monitor. Ouch.

But we never seemed to slam the cell door on Dudley. He'd acted up with us, with US Customs, with his former RCMP colleagues, but nobody with charging authority would ever say, "Fuck this, this isn't funny anymore."

And so, with two weeks to go before I put my papers in, I was out at point when I heard a squeal of tires and the dreaded "It's Dudley."

I was out there with Andy R and Rich, some competent dudes, but I was me, and that meant, I was in charge. I was a victim of my own reputation. In my opinion, both of those dudes were better than me. But I'd become too large for my own boots. Frankly, I was fucking tired.

Dudley pulled up in his SUV, ranting and fucking raving, tossing shit around, apparently in the grip of some sort of psychotic episode. I tried to reason with him and get him to empty his pockets and answer my questions.

It was not to be. "Softly, softly," the UK approach, works only so far with people like Dudley. That is to say, not at all. But it has to be tried. Positive witnessing, and all that.

I'm more of a fan of "Ask, tell, make." Ask them nicely, tell them firmly, make them forcefully. We reached the "tell" stage about twenty seconds in. I told him he was under arrest, for Hindering an Officer. I reached for an arm. He dropped his weight, planting in a fighter's stance.

I pulled him to the ground with my weight, or, as my buddy and use-of-force instructor Alex would call it, "Old Guy Strength." Yeah, it worked, and I came up on top with one cuff on his wrist. But I was lucky not to smash my own brains in on a pillar, as Theresa pointed out to me when she later watched the video.

"I'm planning on it being my last one."

And it was. We didn't charge him that time either, even though there was some dope in the car, too. "Not mine," he said. Of course not.

There are some things I really do miss about the border. But having to take shit from assholes is not one of them. About a month after I'd retired, I was downtown running some errands. I'd stopped for a light on the corner of Burrard and Robson when two magnificent VPD horses and their officers turned the corner on patrol. One of them (the horse, not the officer) took a giant dump.

"Hey!" The scrawny shitrat next to me screamed. "You gonna clean up after that? You guys making messes, all over the city!"

I turned on him. "You probably make more of a mess all on your own, than all the police horses in this city combined, you fucking punk!"

Ahh. It felt good to be a civilian, with the right to an opinion.

Especially when it came to assholes.

FORTY-THREE

THE MAN COMES AROUND

I'd never been much of a union man for the first ten years of my career. Though I had occasionally been badly used by management, more often than not, I ascribed that to my own failings. I knew I had a big mouth, and a tendency to get hot sometimes.

I preferred not to get into long, drawn-hot quarrels with management, though I knew my name was generally not spoken in favourable terms in supervisors' meetings. I had that on good authority.

But my job supplied me with enough conflict. I was paid reasonably well, usually on-time (except on parental leave), and many of my old safety complaints had been addressed by the issuance of firearms. I was fortunate to have had largely sympathetic and competent Superintendents throughout my career, so I rarely had that long-simmering interpersonal conflict that, in my observation, fuelled so many employee grievances.

On top of that, as a life-long political conservative, I was inherently suspicious of unions. Yes, I understood that they had brought about many improvements in the lot of the working man over the years, but the constant stream of left-wing agitation paid for by my union dues grated on me.

When I first came to the border, as funny as it sounds now, many of the old hands regarded me as a possible management spy. That was never true, of course, and I had long ago decided that promotion was simply neither in my cards, nor likely to make me happy.

In 2012, a lot of things happened to make me change my mind. The first was an investigation that turned the formerly credible and relatively untouchable force review process into a travesty. The second was a near-tragedy that garnered a whole lot more attention. After these two events, I was a union man, through and through, although I'd never wave the red banner.

Four officers and one Superintendent were involved in the armed takedown of a vehicle registered to an "armed and dangerous" suspect at Pacific Highway. The vehicle was one in which any number of people could've been hiding themselves, but as it turned out, only the suspect's wife and two kids were on board.

The officers followed their training, to the letter, and detained the individuals on board without incident, then cleared the vehicle. No shots were fired. That would've been the end of it, except that the woman filed a complaint.

I had recently registered myself for shop steward training, having seen from a couple of recent incidents I was involved in personally, that the tide was turning against the officers. Portelance appeared to have a "kick ass" agenda when it came to discipline, and, trained responses or no, a conviction that officers were acting like thugs. I begged to differ.

Therefore, when Dan asked me if I would get involved in the case, I swallowed hard, and said yes. I had no real training for the role, and no idea what I would do. I'd have to make it up as I went along.

The complaint had triggered a Professional Standards investigation, with Internal Investigators being dispatched from Ottawa. The routine force review, carried out by people trained by the RCMP to review such incidents, had concluded that the officers' actions were in keeping with law, policy, and training. The

PSIA investigators had no specialized force review training and were not even qualified to carry firearms themselves.

But the CBSA was not an organization in which ignorance was any bar to interference. The PSIA investigators blundered in like drunks at a wedding reception. Mandated to kick ass, they examined not only what had transpired during the armed encounter, but also rooted through the officers' e-mail accounts, in search of anything which might undermine their credibility.

The day arrived for me to accompany the member I was representing into his interview. He was a mass of nerves, and I was scarcely better. The investigators started out sugary sweet, but quickly went for his jugular. The female was clearly senior, and did most of the talking, but her male sidekick interjected with a snide remark here and then.

This was not a fact-finding mission; it was a prosecutorial attack mission. My "client," if you will, held his own quite well, but every time he referred to his training, she wasn't hearing any of it. She'd push a thick policy binder across the table at him and stab it with her finger. "Show me in here where it says that." Or, "Where is that training in here? Is it here? What page is it?"

I soon tired of her bullshit, and despite the fact I was supposed to be an observer, I had to say something. "Are you going to issue us backpacks to carry those binders around in?" I turned to my client. "Who gave you that training?"

"The CBSA."

I turned back to the investigators. "Maybe you're investigating the wrong guy."

But it didn't matter what we said. The fix was in. The report landed on the desk of the Acting Regional Director. I have it on good authority that the recommendation was; *Fire Everybody.*

I don't know what pressures the A/RD was put under. Maybe the whole thing was a sham, a shot across our bows to reign us in. If it was, it certainly worked, making an already intimidated and demoralized workforce more so.

Luckily, the recommendation was ignored, and everyone kept their jobs. But the bitterness lingered, and I was left with two solid convictions I would keep till the end of my career:

First, the agency was giving us training it didn't believe in or trust. "Follow your training" had become an empty slogan. "Your job or your life" was probably more apt now. Do what will keep you out of trouble, that which the managers want, or follow your training. Protect your life and risk their wrath. Hell of a choice, isn't it?

Second, going along to get along might work on an interpersonal level. But when Ottawa turned its guns on us, we were fools if we didn't fight. I resolved to learn the contract, apply every law and precedent I could, and speak up any chance I got to protect the officers' rights. Submission was suicide. I was still wary of fighting for fighting's sake. But I was damned sure not going to let them crush me, or anyone else, without a fight.

Since Portelance seemed to view me and my colleagues as the enemy, I was happy to be a fly in the ointment. I had decided I could just as easily get fired for doing nothing at all as I could for speaking up. So why not put my big mouth to good use?

I began to study old Labour Relations Board cases. I learned how to instigate Work Refusals. I learned the Grievance process. I made myself known to anyone with a beef. "Hey, you want some representation?" was my "Hello Sailor" line.

Many officers were startled to discover that they had rights at all. Unions had lost a lot of influence in Canadian society since the 1970s, and many of the twentysomething new arrivals had no direct experience or family history with them. So, I, the card-carrying conservative, had to educate them.

Strangely enough, the Chief and the Superintendents were not apparently alarmed. They simply accepted my presence as part of the deal. After all, it was in the contract. It probably helped that I was upfront about not getting drawn into the controversies caused by chronic complainers.

It's probably true in any workplace that 90% of a shop steward's work is focused on 10% of the workforce. These were the lazy, the surly, the incompetent, constantly jousting with the bosses either from resentment, or the fact that their shitty work habits left them a legitimate target of discipline. I did not believe it was my job to indulge their bullshit. I hated working with these people as much as management hated having them in the workforce. I tried to dodge these people whenever I could; and in one case, I flat-out refused to continue representing an officer.

What were they going to do? Fire me from an unpaid job? I got nothing at all, money-wise, for being a shop steward. But I did get to know my rights one hell of a lot better.

Bosses hate grievances. The more they have, the more their bosses wonder, "Can't you manage your people?" So, the system allowed for informal sit-downs before paperwork was filed to resolve a problem. This actually worked a lot of the time, since, like so many human interactions, negative boss/worker encounters were actually the products of a misunderstanding.

Where that didn't work, and in the case of anything involving Ottawa, a grievance was the answer. Sometimes, the results were immediate. Payroll problems for instance, of which there would be more and more thanks to the moronic "Phoenix" pay system, could often be quickly resolved with the mere whisper of the word "Grievance." Yes, they could also take years, but there they sat, unresolved, and festering. Not a good look for ambitious managers.

One thing I had learned about the CBSA: it did not listen to anything, save the politicians who commanded it, and the media who criticized it. That was all. Positive internal change simply was not possible without a public shove.

A tremendous opportunity to shove the agency into change was about to transpire. But it would come at a cost. And then it would be squandered.

FORTY-FOUR
SHOTS FIRED

I wasn't there.

Of all the things that bother me about the shooting of Lori, one of my fellow officers at 13:58 on October 16, 2012, is the fact that I wasn't there.

Would it have changed a single damned thing? Highly unlikely, since on the roster that day were a great many officers whose judgement, initiative, and courage were the equal or the better of mine. If they couldn't change things, why do I think I could?

It's not a rational thought, I suppose. But it remains, like a bad habit. I, who for so long had lectured and thought and drilled for this day, was not there when the ugly reality finally transpired.

But I can't talk about my career at the border without talking about that day.

It began, I suppose, as my shift was ending. At 0600, I filed out of the office, exhausted, walking past the dayshift crew, on their way in. I walked past Lori, a friendly, hard-working newcomer from Ontario.

"Have a good shift." I told her. It would, instead, be a nightmare for her.

There is a certain amount of randomness in law enforcement that challenges the organized mind. No matter how studious or alert one is, the random nature of human behaviour may put one particularly troubled soul on the road to a fatal encounter with you.

You are defined by your uniform and your office. They could be anyone, in an often-swelling crowd of people. They do not know you. But they want you dead, all the same.

I do not know what Andrew Crews, the man who decided to shatter an uneventful afternoon with gunfire, was doing at that exact moment. Had he already decided that he would do what he did? Or did he, too, wake up thinking it was just another day? I have avoided thinking about him for so many years that I really don't know. For a long time, the fact that he was dead was good enough for me.

But death does not bring answers. And Andrew Crews has never given us any.

Fast forward to 1430. I am asleep, alone. Diana and our daughter are in Sao Paulo. She is pregnant with our second daughter. The phone rings, and it's my old friend and fellow CBSA officer Laura.

"Are you okay? You aren't on duty, are you?"

"No. Nightshift, why?"

"Oh no. I hate to have to tell you this, but there was an officer shot at Douglas."

In that instance, two conflicting thoughts merged. "I always knew it would happen." And, "Not another fucking funeral."

"Dead, or alive?"

"I don't know?"

"Suspect?"

"They aren't saying."

These things always happen when I'm sleeping, I thought, thinking back to 9/11. For the sake of world peace, I should be kept awake permanently. At first, I didn't know what to do, thinking I would only be a burden. I decided to go get a coffee and some breakfast. If I couldn't go there, I couldn't wear a hole in the floor at home, either.

I was having breakfast when I decided to call Dan.

"I need you to head over to Pac Highway right now. Dal's over at Douglas with the Mounties. They're diverting all on-duty staff to Pac Highway. Douglas is shut down."

"How bad?"

"One of ours, hit in the neck and shoulder, medivacked to Royal Columbian. Serious but stable."

"Who?"

"Lori, one of the new ones. Not for release. They're having a hard time locating the family."

"Shit. What about the suspect?"

"DOA."

"We shoot him?"

"Don't know yet. Head over there."

I gulped down my coffee, grabbed my badge, and drove to Pacific Highway. So much was going through my mind that it was hard to process. But at least our officer was alive, and the bad guy was dead. That was as good as things could be, in this situation.

I got into Pacific Highway to find an office full of shocked people. I was being asked what was happening, yet I had precious little information. Nobody was especially prepared to take any shit. A traveler acted up during a pocket check, refusing to cooperate, and quickly went nose to toes on the floor.

The Chief of Pac went over, not to apologize on behalf of the Queen, but to point out to the miscreant that today, of all days, was not the day for that shit. Smarten up, asshole.

I spent the day and well into the evening as a sounding board. People knew me, or knew of me, and wanted to talk. Some wanted to cry.

Those of you who don't understand, who think that law enforcement officers should be made of sterner stuff, that they should be ready for such moments, perhaps need reminding that shootings, no matter what Hollywood may show, are rare events. There really is no way, unless such events are happening on a daily or at least weekly basis, to inure oneself.

Sudden, lethal violence directed at someone in your workplace, especially when it appears it could've been anyone, has a way of shaking you up.

There were many declarations of solidarity and "we're all in this together" from Chiefs and Directors that day. An influx of senior bureaucrats from Ottawa, all dressed the way they thought a street cop dressed on his days off should dress, added to the handshakes and solemn promises of change.

I would nod and take it at face value. I knew I was being watched, as a union voice, and as a voice for the senior staff. I hoped the promises and the assurances of solidarity were real and heartfelt.

But I had learned enough about the CBSA to be cautious. And the events of the next day would reinforce that caution tenfold.

After six or so hours at Pacific Highway, I took a call from Kevin, one of the first officers on the scene. I got a more-or-less complete picture of what happened from him.

Kevin was drinking red wine, he said, as he spoke to me. I could imagine, as he spoke, what he saw in the bottom of his glass.

He was on point, in secondary, awaiting his 1400 relief when he heard two shots, in quick succession. Then, a voice, screaming into the radio for help. He put his mic to his mouth.

"Shots fired."

He drew his gun, then moved quickly to an alcove just behind the closest booth to the building, 601. There he met Jessie, and the two were trying to decide whether or not the driver of the white van in 601 was dead or not. He still sat upright in the driver's seat, death metal blasting, even through the closed windows.

Their hand was forced. A rescue party led by Tina was crawling towards 601 to extricate Lori from the line of fire. But they couldn't get into the booth.

The primary booths, then, as now, were locked with Unicam combination locks. In ordinary conditions, these locks are easy to operate. Under extreme combat stress, they are impossible.

Jessie broke cover to help, fumbling it an easy ten times before finally getting in. Kevin went left, joining Gorav and Rich on the other side of the vehicle. Meanwhile, Chris, the Admin Superintendent, and KJ, another line Superintendent on shift, were stacking up a team to clear the vehicle from behind.

Here's the thing that stands out to me: Nobody was running. Nobody abandoned their posts, or fired wildly at the van, or did anything but follow their goddamned training and risk their lives to save their colleague and protect the multitudes of unarmed civilians in the lineup.

Remember that the next time you hear trash talk about border officers. Because a lot of people line up to trash us, including, sometimes, the people we work for.

Kevin decided to break the impasse. He broke out his baton and smashed in the window, then leveled his gun at the driver. "Drop it! Drop the fucking gun! Now!"

Black blood poured out of the driver's mouth, and Kevin knew conclusively he was dead. He'd put the Glock .45 to his head seconds after he shot Lori. Kevin reached across and grabbed the gun.

The others cleared the van, Rich coming up to his wrists in blood and brains, sweating a couple of days of testing before learning he hadn't contracted anything deadly.

Everyone else got an eyeful of things nobody ought to see. A chopper took Lori to the hospital. The officers were sequestered while Homicide was called out. All had to give up their guns and belts, some even their uniforms. Nobody could find a number for Lori's family, until finally they retrieved her cellphone from her locker.

Chris took command of the situation. On that day, and the days to come, he kept the operation glued together, from taking charge of the scene, to managing the aftermath.

The RCMP arrived and shut down the freeway. Nobody could find the bullet that had wounded Lori, until Dal noticed a hole with a deformed slug in it, next to the first aid cabinet. It had ricocheted and changed direction crazily.

Andrew Crews, a tattoo artist and sometime resident of Las Vegas with no criminal history, had driven up from Seattle, sending a final text to his mother: "I love you, I'm sorry." No explanation was ever obtained for what happened next. He pulled up next to 601, where Lori was standing. She asked him to turn down his blaring music. He made to do so, but instead pulled the Glock.

Lori saw the gun and began to move. The bullet went in through her neck and out through her shoulder, taking a crazy, magic bullet detour before lodging in the second window it went into.

Crews put the gun to his head and blew his brains out.

"Are you okay?"

"Me? Oh yeah." Kevin answered, not very convincingly. His call convinced me it was time to go home.

"Pour another glass, bro. You did good today."

FORTY-FIVE
CAREER-LIMITING MOMENT

The next day, we'd set up an impromptu office at the Hazelmere Golf Course on 8th Avenue, as the Pacific Highway crossing would soon be too busy, with Douglas shut down until the investigation was complete.

Honour House, a charitable operation offering accommodation and logistics for the friends and family of wounded law enforcement, emergency services, and military personnel, had opened its doors to us. A number of us wound up there: Trevor and his girlfriend Katie, another CBSA officer, Terry, a shell-shocked yet reassuringly calm Rich and Gorav.

It was good to hang out in the basement on that beautiful early fall day, unwinding in the safe company of each other. We knew it would be bad idea to visit Lori all at once, but we at least hoped to talk to someone from the family, and hand over a card.

But the agency had other plans. Suddenly, a Director and a Chief appeared. I knew them both from the airport. "Say guys, it's really great that you're here to support Lori," the Director started off, "But the family really doesn't want her to be disturbed at this time."

You really could've heard a pin drop at that point. Here was this rear-echelon motherfucker trying to evict us, including two people who'd literally been up to their wrists in blood the day before, after the people from Honour House had welcomed us with open arms. I could see a vein bulging in Trevor's head.

"Is that what the family said?" I finally asked.

"What? Well, they've just expressed a wish that she not be bothered..."

"So, who's bothering her? You've got a bunch of her co-workers here, including a couple who were there when it went down, unwinding in each other's company. Honour House is all about that, right?"

"We're not going anywhere." Trevor chimed in.

Just then, the Chief started trying to take surreptitious photos with his cell phone.

"Are you taking photos?" Terry asked.

"Hey, listen, I'll tell you what. Why don't you send somebody from Honour House to kick us out? It's their house. Not yours." I smiled insincerely.

The Director stammered. "Well, I am a representative of the agency, and..."

"And what? We're all off duty. Like you always remind us, we're private citizens when we're off duty. And since you're not enforcing any border legislation right now, so are you."

They beat a hasty retreat. "Whew." Terry exhaled. "That was a career limiting moment."

"Fuck 'em." Trevor cursed. "I'm not taking their shit."

When they returned with the lady from Honour House, perhaps they weren't expecting what she had to say. "You're all welcome to stay down here for as long as you want."

"Why thank you." I smiled at her.

That was the first indication that the agency was up to their usual shit. Nothing had changed. They'd thrown a phalanx of managers around Lori, controlling access. By the next day, our Director was proclaiming that nothing could've prevented Lori's shooting, whether not she had ballistic protection, or a gun on her hip. 65% of the staff were still unarmed, as managing summer lineups still took precedence over arming seats. And of course, recall the laughter that had greeted my suggestion of ballistic glass.

I became deeply involved in the after-action review, representing the union. I wanted to explore what would've happened if Crews had been a better armed, more determined opponent. The agency wanted to deal only with the status quo, like an army that prepares only for the last war it fought.

In the middle of all of this, I got devastating news from Brazil. Diana had gone for a checkup, and no fetal heartbeat had been discovered. We'd lost the baby.

I think she was surprised how much I cried about it, as I hadn't been too enthusiastic at first about having another child. But on top of everything that had just happened, I needed a hopeful sign. It all just seemed too cruel.

The port reopened, KJ taking the symbolic first road time in 601. Some took longer than others to come back to work. Some suffer to this day. Lori made a full physical recovery.

I made a number of recommendations to the unprecedented Labour Canada investigation into the shooting. Among them were:

-long guns available for similarly armed assailants
-Tasers for use with less-lethal threats and EDP (Emotionally Disturbed Persons)
-Ballistic protection in the booths
-Radios with improved range, and interoperability with the ECOMM dispatch system

-Improved tactical training

It seemed that things might change. I was cautiously hopeful, especially considering that an outside agency was holding the CBSA's feet to the fire, to their obvious displeasure.

I was also encouraged by new news from Brazil: My wife had trusted her instincts and gone back for another checkup. This time, there was a heartbeat. We would have a new arrival after all.

Time would tell if the CBSA would learn anything from the shooting. A lot more time than I was expecting. Legislation required them to share the final report and recommendations of a workplace hazard investigation as soon as they received them with the workplace Operational Health and Safety Committee, of which I was now the union representative.

But they "lost" the report, for eighteen goddamned months. Probably because the report was quite enthusiastic about ballistic protection in the booths. No more laughter. But there was some fear, since in my world, you don't lose and forget about a report like that.

It only came to life after I asked about it in an OHS Committee meeting one day.

Six years after the shooting, I finally received a response to my Information Act request for all documents relating to the CBSA to the investigation. I passed the heavily redacted and largely uninformative package along to the union with a pointed query about whether or not anyone still gave a shit. I never got a reply.

It has now been almost eight years since the shooting. None of the substantive recommendations I made were implemented. Most of Labour Canada's were ignored.

It has been nearly eight years since the last shooting of a largely defenceless officer at a border crossing. Since the CBSA has done nothing but congratulate itself since this time, it is anyone's guess how long it will be until there is another.

Perhaps this time, it will be the airport, where the officers are almost all trained to carry firearms, but where those firearms are locked up. The active shooter plan there consists of hiding and waiting for the real police. God forbid anyone should draw a gun they are trained to use.

Perhaps it will be an Inland office, where officers may only carry when they are going out on the road. Surely, nobody upset over an immigration decision will ever kill the unarmed Commissionaire guarding the door and take it out on the unarmed people inside.

The agency seems more afraid of the people they have working for them, than the people who hate us. This despite the fact that, in the thirteen years that border officers have been carrying guns, not a single shot has been fired at a human being.

So, what are they afraid of, after all?

FORTY-SIX

WASHINGTON!

Whatever other tides might have swept across the border in that time, one thing never changed: The ever-lingering potential for sudden, unexplained chaos.

The nut magnet that was Pacific Highway had lost none of it's pull.

Sometimes, the incidents left you laughing. Other times, they left you chilled to the bone.

I was coming off the line one sunny day when I heard a vehicle pull away at speed from another booth. "See that guy?" Dave, of the Million-Dollar Minivan fame, was now my acting Superintendent. "Can you go help Jose before someone gets killed?"

The little car had now pulled up next to Jose, a large, bald Mexican who used to work corrections, and was not exactly known for suffering fools gladly. The driver was a silver-haired white man, and he was screaming at the top of his lungs. I ran over, arriving just as Jose had made his "fuck this shit" decision, and had wrenched open the driver's side door.

I reached into the car and grabbed the driver's outstretched arm. Luckily, people who have a problem with law enforcement also usually have a problem wearing their seatbelts. He came out easily, and Jose and I wrestled him to the ground.

The only problem was, the car was in gear, and the rear wheels missed my ankles by inches. Paul jumped into the driver's seat and stopped the car. We got the cuffs on and pulled the driver to his feet. Blood ran down his forehead and face.

Here's a sneaky tip for you, the next time some lawyer gets on TV squawking about how the police brutally beat his client, and having the photos to prove it: Usually, the injuries are inadvertent, caused by the unfortunate failure of the authorities to put soft, foamy mats on every exposed hard surface. You see, we're trained to end fights quickly by taking people to the ground. The ground is hard.

The first words out of his mouth were "I'm a lawyer." Oh, great.

We took him in on his outstanding Mental Health warrant. He later, surprisingly, apologized. I wish him well. Sometimes, when the fight's over, you realize you were just there on a person's worst day, and things escalated too quickly to talk them down. That's another thing you should remember when people say the police need "more training" to deal with the mentally ill. All the training in the world will not put the stopper in a volcano. We prefer to talk. But we have to stop them from hurting anyone, including themselves.

Sometimes, we could prevent damage, at least temporarily. I was working with Jose another time when we stopped a young man on his way to Alaska and searched him for guns. He hadn't declared any, but our search uncovered a couple of handguns. We arrested him, and as we were finishing up our search, Jose found a suicide note.

The young man was going to drive to Alaska, find a quiet place (not hard to do up there), and shoot himself. We took him at his word and escorted him back to US Customs without laying charges, with the suggestion that maybe a mental health evaluation was in order. Other than taking his guns, that was all we could do.

Maybe we convinced him somebody cared. Maybe he did it anyway. I'll never know.

Sometimes, the suicidal were depending on us to do the job for them. I was out in secondary one evening when Kendy, searching a Ryder truck next to me, shouted in alarm. She'd opened the roll door to find a tall, emaciated man hiding under blankets. She drew down on him and ordered him out. Josh and I got him cuffed, then I drew and cleared the back of the truck at gunpoint.

Right where Kendy had found him hiding were two nasty-looking makeshift swords. Five minutes after we got him into cells, he was smashing his own head on the toilet and screaming "Kill me!"

One thing I've learned about extreme mental illness: One minute they're fine, or seemingly so. The next minute, they're not. Had Kendy opened that roll door five minutes later, we might've been forced to shoot that man. God only knows.

Another time, the RCMP dropped a prisoner off with us for return to the US. We were doing the handover when he began screaming "Shoot me! Shoot me you fucking pigs!"

I reminded him that his timing was off. "You're handcuffed and shackled, and you've been searched five times since breakfast. Why would I shoot you?"

He might've been crazy, but he wasn't stupid. He stopped yelling.

Sometimes, what seems crazy is merely desperate. I was walking in for an afternoon shift when I found a post-incident conference just breaking up. Clearly, something big had just gone down, but at that stage of my career, it didn't involve me, and nobody was dead, so who gave a shit?

"The training kicked in!" The Chief of Pac Highway gave me one of his trademark overpressure handshakes.

"Okay. Good to hear."

I got the crazy story later. A male driving an Oregon-plated vehicle had been referred for exam. Sukh went out to search the car, then found himself in the middle of what seemed at first like a hostage standoff.

A male and a female were hiding in the back of the station wagon, and the male had a knife with a concealed blade. It appeared that he was holding her hostage. Sukh, and Ruby, the acting Superintendent, began a dialogue with him. An RCMP unit showed up. Jim was showing a rookie around and provided lethal overwatch.

What had actually happened is that the two in the car had been involved in a wild chase with police two days earlier, in which a police dog had been shot. Now, they were trying desperately to negotiate their way out of a dead-end situation.

When there's time; when there's distance; we talk.

Somehow, the talk worked, the male tried to exit, and was taken down. It was a classic example of another jurisdictions' shit winding up at the border. American fugitives are always drawn to Canada, often incorrectly believing that they can be left alone, if only they make it across the line. Hollywood has let a lot of people down.

A poor decision involving a gun at the border can create its own crisis. I was working point one day when I saw a male in a Washington-plated car driving hesitantly and erratically towards me. "Watch this guy closely" the primary officer radioed.

When he pulled up at the stop sign, he was bent over, fucking with something under his floormats. My hand went to my gun. "Hands! I want to see hands!" I radioed for backup. The driver straightened up. "Shut it off and step out."

"I was only..."

"NOW!"

The driver hurried to exit. I brought him back to the trunk and frisked him. "What were you fucking with down there?"

"Ah...I'm sorry. I forgot I had a knife."

"That's all, huh? A knife?"

"Yes sir."

"We'll see. Go inside and sit down."

"But my car..."

"Is going to be searched by us. Go sit down."

The two officers who searched the car were not exactly deep concealment experts. Eventually Jessie and Cory threw their hands up in despair and came out to search the car. They found the pistol behind the driver's seat. The driver had taken his concealed pistol off and tossed it behind the seat, then was trying to hide a magazine when I saw him pulling up.

If he'd had that gun in his hand when he drove up...I knew how quickly an officer could be shot, and I did not intend to be the next one.

Three of my colleagues at Pacific Highway came even closer to finding out. Bryce and Jon were checking a vehicle that smelled of dope at primary. They had the driver pop the trunk, whereupon Jon found the box for a Glock. Bryce ordered the driver out, but he went for the Glock instead.

A hand-to-hand struggle began, and when Jon came around the corner, seeing his partner fighting with an armed man, he drew down, and decided to fire.

Then, Bryce made the suspect lose his grip. The Glock went flying, and the suspect decided to run, headed right for a rookie officer, who drew his gun, convinced the driver was gunning for him, forcing the driver to swerve.

After a crazy pursuit which ended kilometres away in Langley, and after tossing his gun, the suspect was finally caught with a bag of dope in the trunk.

Sometimes, the encounters were just plain bizarre. So it was with Washington. Washington's family had decided to bring him back to Canada so his increasingly obvious mental illness could be treated. But, as the border approached, Washington decided he wanted to stay in...well, Washington.

He leapt out of the family car in the border lineup and tried to carjack the car ahead of him. Jessie and Paul were ahead of me as we ran out to the scene. There was a struggle as the unfortunate young man, screaming "Washington!" was manhandled inside the office.

Once he was in cells, Washington decided to turn over a new leaf. He calmly stripped off all of his clothes, then began a vigorous set of pushups.

Paul and I stood outside the cell door, watching.

"Why are we watching this?" I wondered aloud.

"I've been looking for a new workout. It's important to stay in shape in the joint." Paul replied. His workout finished, Washington stood and began to masturbate vigorously.

Jim was watching too. "Hey!" he yelled, "What are you doing?"

"Just playing with my balls, sir!"

"Okay. You keep on playing with your balls."

"Washington!" Washington screamed.

FORTY-SEVEN
TACTICAL WITHDRAWAL

Technically, the "retirement process" is simply a series of steps that commences when you decide to submit a letter of resignation to the agency.

There are forms to be filled out, pension options to be chosen, things to be turned in, a retirement party to be planned. It's a process, all right.

Legally speaking, this process would not begin for me for another four years. But actually, it began in 2013.

I prefer to consider it a "tactical withdrawal," and, like that silly, use-of-force non-option from the days before guns, it telegraphed the user's intentions grandly. I was officially in the Honourable Order of Get Someone Else to Fucking Do It.

I'd made up my mind: I wasn't going to make it to full pension, which for me, would come sometime at the age of 61. 61? How the fuck could I put up with this shit for another 17 years? I'd be clearing *flying* cars by the time I retired.

I'd read some depressing statistics about people who stayed at their posts. *They died.* If you left at age 60, apparently, you could expect to live until age 80. If you hung on like a leech until you were 65, you wouldn't even enjoy two summers in Palm Springs. You'd be dead by 67.

Every time I had to take somebody down, I got up a little slower. Every triennial recertification was dreaded. "I'll catch up to you" became my favourite catch phrase.

On top of all that, the work was less fun than it used to be. The division of labour between Immigration and Customs was so slanted that I could, in any given week, expect to spend less than 25% of my time doing what I was good at, and what I liked. And if I had a brain fart and left my gun locker open? I could get ten days on the fucking beach. First offence.

Field training was a thing of the past, and we returned to "pass the new guy around." I no longer cared. If I was the pariah so many on the top floor seemed to think I was, then me training new people would training them to fail.

I found a booth in the office and sat there. "You know where to find me" became another catch phrase.

I felt alone, especially when one of the people I really trusted wasn't there. In sharp contrast to ten years before, my way of doing things was now the minority report. I stopped trying to correct the junior officers' shitty tactics. I began to characterize officers into two groups: Those of whom I'd back up; and those who would have me seeking something big and solid to hide behind until they were finished.

The new recruit program in Rigaud was longer, more paramilitary, and supposedly more related to what we actually did. The first couple of classes were actually fairly good. Then things began to slip.

The problem was, in 2014 a general wave of anti-police sentiment began to sweep North America. Law enforcement lost prestige and became perceived as too dangerous for the money. Plus, the economy was in recovery mode, and a civil service job was no longer the sure lure it used to be. So, suddenly we were fighting with the city forces and the RCMP for recruits. The city forces paid the best and trained close to home. The RCMP? Well, whatever its current problems, it was still the RCMP. Little kids did not grow up dreaming of being CBSA officers. They sure as hell all wanted to be Mounties.

Eventually, we began to see the effects. Stupidly, the managers had implemented a cadet pay system, similar to the one the RCMP had already abandoned. Then, they got rid of the best test scores/top pick of postings system that had given Douglas an initial wave of quality officers and replaced it with a randomized posting system.

If you were a kid from Toronto, and no matter how hard you worked in Rigaud, your reward might be a posting to Big Beaver, SK, would you try that hard? Or would you walk and take your training to Metro Toronto or the OPP at the first opportunity?

It's a rhetorical question, of course. We couldn't get as many good ones as we once did, and those we got, we often couldn't retain. Increasingly, the default comment on many recruits' files was "How the fuck did he get here?"

All of these problems were far from my mind as my wife and I welcomed our second daughter in Brazil. I began to think of myself as living in Brazil, maybe provisionally going back…perhaps.

I began writing around this time, too. I would take an iPad to Horto Florestal, a tree-lined lake complete with Howler Monkeys, and type away in the blistering sun. Or, I'd prop up a table at a corner bar, drinking caipirinhas and eating *frango galeto* while writing.

It was a first attempt, and it was a mess. But I would get better.

More important, my identity was changing. I was no longer a lifer. I began to wonder what a life on the beach with a laptop would be like. There was no more longing to go back to a job that was really no longer there. Not like last time.

When I got back, I went for my three-year recertification at

Rigaud. It would be the last visit of my career. I had to say, I was impressed. The recruits were sharp-looking, squared-away, and respectful. If you didn't have a red "cadet" tab on your epaulettes, you got called "sir," or "ma'am." The facilities were upgraded, including two 18-lane shooting ranges, constantly kept clean by running water, which had the unfortunate effect of always making you want to pee, rather than concentrate on your shooting.

Best of all, I was seeing Quebec at its riotous fall best. 20 C afternoons, with leaves in almost every colour of the rainbow. It almost made me want to stay.

That week in Rigaud made me think. The CBSA had the potential for positive change. Gone was the slovenly character of the recruits of old, the drinking in the hallways, the lack of respect. I liked the new Rigaud better.

But why wasn't this translating into improvements in the field? Was it too late to revive the beast?

And more to the point, why should I care? I had one foot out the door already. My tactical withdrawal had begun.

FORTY-SEVEN

ON DUTY/OFF DUTY

Anyone who has been in law enforcement for a few years, or who is married to anyone who has, will notice a change.

Your formerly laid-back spousal unit goes from being the average, "Hey, let's hang out at Bed, Bath, and Beyond", to being "Ready yourselves for the end times."

It's inevitable. And it can't be helped. Ask anyone. Long before I signed up with CBSA, security work had ruined me. My first wife got to the point where she couldn't stand my hypervigilance in any public space.

Who's that? Do I know him? Have I arrested him for something? Will he have a beef?

This hypervigilance, this need to always have one's head on a swivel; this was the real cause of so much cop trauma. Don't take it from me; take it from Dr Keith Gilmartin, a former cop and a psychologist, author of the landmark text, *Emotional Survival for Law Enforcement*.

I had the privilege to attend a seminar put on by Gilmartin, and, in a rare enlightened gesture by the CBSA, paid for by them, for both officers and spouses. He put a central question to us:

"When you hear the phrase, 'Boy Scout Troop Leader,' what's the first thing you think?"

"Pedophile!" We all shouted in unison, while wives and girlfriends looked on in mute horror.

"You know," He paused, "98% of cops say that. You know how many civilians do? 2%."

Certain knowledge taints you with the knowing of it. Knowing how to kill. Knowing how people deceive in order to betray the most scared trusts. These are like atomic bomb secrets, the corruption of matter to produce genocide, and they cannot be undone. Gilmartin convinced me then, and nobody has ever convinced me otherwise, that these pressures, these chronic stresses, are far more deadly than the blood and guts trauma we believe kill so many cops.

The cop immerses himself in corruption, then returns home and must depressurize, like the diver returning from the bathos. He finds his "magic chair," and his "magic elixir," usually alcohol, and thus can he reintegrate into society.

I was not alone amongst many of my colleagues. I would tell my stories and see people's faces freeze over. So soon, I would stop telling them. I would tell them only to people who had the code. To the people who had the magic chair.

Finally, I understood my father, who had kept so much locked up for so long. He told me a few things. Things I didn't want to know, like how murder victims had died. But I needed to take that knowledge off his shoulders, not because I would ever tell you (I wrote a book about it, and I still won't say shit) but because no cop should carry this load without his partner shouldering it with him. It's just not done. My father had always wanted to ride with me for at least one shift; this was the least I could do for my mentor and my hero.

It's too late for my dad. He fought for years to get the Force to acknowledge the reality of PTSD, of the dead bodies, the hostage takings, the riots, the decision to kill and then it's relenting. Finally, they gave him a pension for it, but by then, he was broken.

My father gave, if not his life, then at least, his mind and spirit for his country.

But it wasn't too late for me, so I figured. I had faced only the light version of my dad's experiences, so I figured. I was not programmed for a life of hypervigilance.

The year I retired from the CBSA; I got an ironic wake-up call.

My father, 76 years old, was returning from a visit to the tall ships in Steveston harbour with my stepmother, when he witnessed a man pounding on a woman's windshield, terrifying her, and ripping off her windshield wipers.

A cop's training dies hard. My father stepped out and knocked the motherfucker on his ass.

I was proud, of course, but perversely certain that was not me. My father had loved the RCMP, even when it was vigorously fucking him over; I had no such love for the CBSA.

A year later, in Sao Paulo. I was walking home, alone. Two cops had a car stopped, tense, waiting for cover. I made eye contact with them, slipping behind them into an alley, watching their backs.

They nodded to me, knowingly. "You've got this?"

"Car to cover. Show me 10-6." I nodded back.

It never goes away. Don't ever sign up if you think you want to walk away. If you care, you never will. Never.

My father lives in a care facility now, most of his mind, gone. You know what part is left?

The watching part. The nurses tell me, he walks the halls at night, looking out for the other patients. They call him "The Policeman," because that is the part that will never die.

Once you put that badge on, you'd better be prepared. If you're like me; if you're like my dad, you'll never get it off. There is no "off duty," you hear me?

That's okay. That's the part I never want to leave behind. I never wanted to be a victim, anyway.

FORTY-EIGHT

HOT WEATHER AND FULL MOONS

Okay, scientists. You're going to call bullshit on this. But every boy and girl walking a tier, manning a booth, or pushing a black and white out there tonight knows a few immutable truths:

-Shit floats
-Payday is Wednesday
-Hot weather breeds violence
-Full moons spawn craziness

Tell me I'm wrong. No, I am not looking at you, Mr Social Science Major. I am looking at someone with a bad back from wearing all that fucking gear and a Kevlar vest for twenty years. You'll agree with me.

You see, every time there was a full moon overhead, or the thermometer got over 25C, everyone got that edgy look in the locker room; like it was game on. Hell, I used to do stretches and shadow box. Because you just knew that someone was going to take a piece out of you.

Managers, that is to say, *rational people*, would of course disagree. They dwell in the rational world of stats, flattened over the course of months and years. They have not worked those July and August nights, nights so hot and urgent that when you take your vest off at the end of them you can feel ever bone in your body aching; nights when your own stink overwhelms you; nights when you can't wait to get to home, so you step across the street for choir practice, Code 3.

I remember those nights. Perhaps those are the most vivid of all.

Working the Old Douglas, one night, on primary, when an ungodly scream emanates from the office. I unass my booth, snap out the stick, run for the sound. Jim and Jason are searching one of my referrals, some tightly wound survivalist freak from Utah, who suddenly decides he's not with the program and decides to run screaming out to secondary. Emilie is chasing him, her baton out, and soon we're squared off with him, Jason sneaking up on him from behind, when Jim just calmly walks up and slaps the cuffs on him.

He didn't have anything, you see. It was just…hot. It gets to people.

Like the freak with the U-Haul full of dildos and bondage gear. This cat pulls up on a hot summer day, moving to Canada, his momma waiting for him. Too bad he's got underage nudies in his computer. That's when Tina tells me to slap the irons on him, and, of course, momma jumps on my back, screaming and clawing, and Julie jumps on her back, protecting her partner, and soon I've got 300 pounds on an already fucked-up spine.

So, I start smearing a Farsi-screaming momma off on the side of a U-Haul, while my partner tries to rip her off my back, and dildos are falling out of the fucking tailgate. You cannot make this shit up.

Join the CBSA, kids. Be all you can be.

The park traffic, of course, heats up with the weather. In cool weather, the question, "Hey, what's up?" Is only answered by "You're under arrest" 25% of the time. In summer, it shoots up to fifty.

Zombies multiplied in hot weather. Zombies were people who seemed to believe that ignoring the nice policeman would make him go away. Responding to a call from Border Patrol, I humped over a hedge with Theresa hot on my heels to intercept a Zombie trucking north.

He was almost two-dimensional; he was so tall and skinny. He pretended I wasn't there until I upended him on his face. He'd been told "no," so he decided to pretend we, and by extension, the border, didn't exist.

We fought people in rose gardens, chased them into people's yards, dragged them out of bathrooms. Sweating in midnight blue uniforms, soaking under Kevlar, radios dragging behind us, falling on our faces.

Sometimes, those summer nights, I would sit on a bench for twenty minutes before I could move a muscle. Other times, I would wipe the blood off my handcuffs, spray them with disinfectant, and pray I wouldn't take anything home to my family.

"I've got AIDS! Now you fuckers all got it too!"

I remember when that shit used to scare me. Now I just sprayed everything twice. *Whatever.*

"I ain't sitting down. Fuck you." He was 6'3, solid, and pissed off. I can't remember what I'd arrested him for. I guess it was a gun.

"Dude, you are sitting down, or I can't leave this cell. Sit your ass down."

"Fuck you, ofay."

The fingers down into the sternum, they settled every argument. Big and tall, they cried like a baby.

Listen: it's not about power and control, okay? It's about survival. We'd all been seen the videos in training, other cops on hot summer nights, ignoring the signs of defiance; paying with their lives.

Defiance is deadly. Defiance is a warning sign. Soon, you'll be fighting for your life.

Kyle Dinkheller. We all remembered that one. A southern deputy, he pulled over the wrong man one day, and paid with his life. I thought about him a lot, when I encountered defiance.

We'd all seen the dashcam video. We'd all heard his screams. And every summer night, when we dealt with the defiant and the violent, we all determined: *Not me. Not tonight.*

So, there were a lot of fights. The janitors were busy. But complaints were few. We picked the right fights, and most of our opponents disappeared into the justice system on either side of the border, where they belonged.

After a night shift, I'd sit on my balcony at 0630, nursing a cold one, almost relishing one of my neighbours looking across the way and thinking; "Oh, that poor man."

Lady, you don't know the half of it.

FORTY-NINE

MORE GUNS, AND OTHER THINGS ON WHICH PAPERWORK IS GENERATED

My interest level might have been in decline, but the job still presented many options to pass the time. In my last few years, I was fortunate. My working environment was as easy as it could've been.

I had a Superintendent, Jessie, who had started at the airport a short time after me, and who understood my style very well. Though I was sure I sometimes exasperated him, I always had the feeling that he had my back. He was an officer's supervisor, the kind of guy who would support you if you were doing the right thing. I let him know early on I was on the downward slide. But I also told him I would keep putting in the effort, as long as the Queen kept paying me.

Jessie left me alone to do what I knew how to do. In return, I tried to keep his migraines to a minimum.

A new shift bid system favoured seniority. This benefited me, by now the second-most senior line officer at the POE, in two ways: First, I got dibs on what team I wanted. Second, I got to work with other old hands, one of whom, Graydon, I knew would gladly take my graveyards.

I was too old for graveyards. Plus, I got to work with Jim again, and, in conjunction with a decent crew of younger officers, this made me happy as I could be.

Also, there was a fuck of a lot of money lying around on the table. I am talking overtime, hermano. I worked two straight years where my salary plus OT was more than a Chief's base pay. I knew a couple guys who were making more than Vice-Presidents.

But Jesus, was it exhausting. After my close call in the alley with the biker, I calmed down a bit.

I didn't have to chase my tail as much as some of the other officers. Jim and I still generated stats, so we were freer than most to write them up. One thing about working at a place like Douglas: it's a generalist's heaven.

Lots of people dream of working on one specific thing; guns, drugs, gangs, whatever. Not me. I liked the roulette wheel aspect of line work, where you could be working an immigration case one day, a drunk driver the next, then a warrant or a breach, and then a smuggled car.

People never stopped lying. That kept us in business. And on Team Three, I was, if not as free in the Golden Age, at least a little free to do what I liked, and what I was good at.

I was about to kick back an American citizen of Somali birth for a criminal conviction when he said, "Oh, no, listen, I'm a Canadian."

"Oh, really?"

"Yeah. Just, uh, you know. Not under this name."

"Aha. Turn around and put your hands behind your back." Word to the wise: DO NOT fuck with identity at the border. It gives an officer tremendous latitude to detain you until he can find out exactly who you are.

Turns out, this cat had outsmarted himself. The man he claimed to be had in fact been accepted as a refugee at the age of twelve.

At age eighteen, he decided that life in Toronto wasn't exciting enough, so he went to San Francisco, and mailed all his ID back home. Then, he made a refugee claim as a Somali citizen under a different name.

Pretty sure the song said, "wear a flower in your hair." Not that other shit. But, okay. Now the only problem was, dude's family hated him now, and said "Ahmed who?" when we called. And the Immigration file from way back when? No fingerprints, and only a photocopy of a picture of an unsmiling black person with their eyes closed. You get the picture, right?

The Immigration and Refugee Board were not impressed, for once: DEPORTED.

Maybe he was a Canadian. I don't know. But I'm not the one who chose to be a fucking liar to game the system. He wasn't running from Somalia when he did it, either. He was running from Toronto.

Odds are the Americans punted him back to Somalia: high nineties. Now THAT's fucking up an opportunity.

Two yokels, one kid not really related to them. Twenty-six guns, prohibited weapons, and or imitations thereof. That's planet OH-10 for you. Ohio is the vortex of some weird forces in the US. Though not technically in the South, it is as snaggle-toothed a place as any I've ever seen, its inhabitants making people from Georgia look like Old Etonians.

Actually, most people from Georgia are nice. They have manners.

These yokels were nice enough, I guess, except they forgot to mention that their crapped out 70s van was sagging under the weight of AR-15s, pistols, rifles, shotguns, and other stuff for the hurting of peoples. Plus, the kid. Never really figured out where he came from. Left that one to the Americans, frankly. But it made for a nice trophy shot.

Cubans. Cubans are...well, I am sure there are lots of nice Cubans. I have to remind myself that they were not typically the ones we got to deal with.

Two cases in point:

One day, we caught a call of a suspicious vehicle lurking on Zero Avenue, with a couple of males on their way from the US to meet up with it. Border Patrol was watching, but I think they must've already known they were Cubans, because they were strictly hands-off. You can bet, if they thought the Montana brothers' backpacks were full of yayo, we'd have never gotten near them.

Two things that need explaining: One, Zero Avenue is the literal border. And homes are built right up to it. It's a nightmare to police. And according to our agreement with the RCMP, we were not really supposed to be doing the policing. But the law allowed it. Ray, one of the Superintendents, and I, jumped in a car and went after them.

Another thing: The US kind of have to let all kinds of Cubans in. It's a political thing. But once they fuck up, like getting felony prison sentences, they're happy to shunt them north, which was probably why Border Patrol was not running interference that day. I told you we never meet the nice Cubans.

Ray and I didn't always see eye-to-eye. But one thing I liked about him was his willingness to look for trouble off the port. Soon, we saw the vehicle BP dispatch had reported. I lit them up.

I started pulling IDs, then we snared the two Cubans crossing the ditch. We ran indices on all of them. All here on refugee claims, from the States, which meant that's where they weren't supposed to go. Three out of five with violent felony records. Three out of five "armed and dangerous."

They got to see mami in Florida. And there was fuck all we could do about it, even though they'd breached their terms. Why? The Americans never made them citizens, and so don't have to take them back. The Cubans dump their unwanted prison populations on Uncle Sam and won't ever give any of them travel documents to come home.

Canada plays nice. And, as usual, takes it in the ass. Another example of this occurred one cold night.

A Hispanic lady in an SUV with New Mexico plates showed up. Her story was obvious bullshit, and she lived close to the big bad border, so I sent her in.

But when I dealt with her in the office, I began to suspect she wasn't a liar of the malicious variety. I approached her with Treena, an officer with a great empathetic approach (better than mine, which isn't saying much).

"Listen. I know you're not being straight with me. But I also know you're not a bad person. So, help me sort this out, okay?"

"Okay."

We escorted her to a private interview room and let her compose herself. Then it all came out.

She'd shacked up with a Cuban guy the year previously. Then, her sixteen-year old daughter alleged that the guy had raped her. This wasn't hard to believe, since he'd just done a ten-year jolt for rape in state prison. She went to the cops, and he bolted. The lady remembered he had a brother who lived in Surrey, and the detectives in Santa Fe suggested she come up for a look so they could get a warrant.

Thanks for calling us, pendejos. "Let us handle this." I called Inland Enforcement and asked them to come down. In the meantime, I found an address for the brother in Surrey, and guess who was wanted on an Immigration warrant?

Yes, Inland went around there, and yes, they arrested the Scum

Brothers there in their underwear.

But, like I told you before, we never get rid of Cubans.

Wrong turns continued to reward me. There was the Washington State pot dealer, high on his own supply, who'd taken a wrong turn looking for the last exit into Blaine. After I took a couple of fistfuls of dope off of him in the office, I went out to the car, pulled a jacket off the back seat, and found an AK-47 and 12 GA shotgun laid casually across the rich Corinthian leather.

All-righty then.

Another time, it was a rolling felony stop from the Canadian side. They had no clue, and no ID save two inmate cards from Mission Institution. Miraculously, the car was not stolen.

The back-seat passenger had no idea. He was a scrawny little worm.

"So, where's your ID then?"

"Don't have any."

"What's your name?"

He gave me one, but he must've had a head injury or something, because he was awfully hesitant. "You sure, now?"

"Of course, I am. Ha ha."

"Okay. Just remember that giving a policeman a false name is serious crime. Especially at the border. So, this is your name, and date of birth, right?"

"Uh, yes."

"And you understand that I will arrest you if it isn't, right?"

"Sure."

Two minutes into the vehicle search, I found a photocopy of his BC ID stuffed under a seat. Different name, different DOB. I took it inside the office. I like playing show and tell.

"Look what I found."

"Oh."

"Remember what I told you?"

"Yes." He assumed the position. "Does this mean I'm going back to jail now?"

"Yup."

He couldn't say I didn't warn him.

Another rolling felony stop showed up at the POE on a busy Saturday night. A precipitous increase in the value of the Canadian dollar versus the US had led to crazy lineups of cross-border shoppers.

That meant lots of OT for us, and the desperate recruitment of officers from other divisions, some of whom were not very street smart. In their areas, they didn't have to be.

One such sort was in 601 that very minute, about to send three shitrats my way with a Saturday Night Special in a Burger King bag, while I, at point, tried to manage an ambulance, a fire truck (attending a medical emergency), and all the other shoppers coming and going. I got on the air.

"No, disarm them right there. Do not send that car over here, do you hear me?"

Chris K and another officer hurried out and took the gun. The transplant never worked with us again, although I hear he never understood how he fucked up. Which makes me doubly glad he never worked at Douglas again.

I could keep going. But you probably want to hear about murder most foul, don't you?

Of course, you do. It's a trip. It's the biggest collar there is. And once I got it, however inadvertently, there was nothing keeping me from leaving. Nothing but time, and money.

FIFTY

MURDER, HE TEXTED

Many law enforcement officers will never solve a homicide in their careers, or even arrest someone connected with a homicide.

My father was a very active and aggressive policeman, and although he did take down a homicidal sniper at gunpoint, early in his career, VPD stole the collar from him. So, technically, he never made a homicide arrest.

I never really expected to solve a murder. That's not typically a CBSA officer's job. But, one night in the summer of 2014, I kind of stumbled into it.

Now I really mean, *stumbled.* When I say, "I solved a murder," please understand, this is not Sherlock Holmes here, and my quarry was not Professor Moriarty. My ability to "solve" this murder was really down to three things: My luck, his stupidity, and S.99 of the *Customs Act.*

Remember that border legislation authorizes very broad searches of people, vehicles, and cargo at the international border, routinely and without warrant. This is in stark contrast to domestic law enforcement, where these days doing anything beyond waving and smiling at a suspect requires written consent or a warrant.

For some reason, while they are hell-bent on hamstringing street cops, Canadian judges are far less sanguine about the prospects of a wide-open border. CBSA officers have it pretty easy when it comes to search and seizure.

This is, of course, not without some controversy. Lawyers would love to smash open the golden egg of border searches, to find some crack into which they could wedge themselves, thereby making millions on Charter challenges of border law. So far, the courts have resisted this.

But, the advent of widespread personal electronic devices may be that wedge. Many people now empty their entire lives into their smartphones. Private chats, intimate pictures, banking information, GPS tracking of where they took their holiday snaps...it's all up for grabs the second we get into your phone.

Because S.99 of the *Customs Act*, written in the days when a computer was something that needed its own building, never anticipated this reality, a smartphone is a "good" like any other. And so, we may look into it. There are many good reasons to allow officers to do this. For instance, who really wants child pornographers to be able to swan across the line with their foul images unchecked? Drug smugglers sending messages to each other to coordinate their efforts; we should be able to catch them, right? How about people lying about their vacation, while actually coming in to steal Canadian jobs? Terrorists with their vile ISIS videos?

That's why we pry into your privacy. But there's no doubt that it gets problematic sometimes. It bothered me to see officers snickering over someone's home-made, consensual pornography. I preferred a flick through as fast as possible until you see something bad approach. Most of what's in other people's phones really is none of our business. But how to find the bad stuff, without looking at the innocuous chaff?

Eventually, the CBSA would act to discourage its officers from routine examination of electronic devices. Lucky for me, and the citizens of Washington State that this decision was made after that summer night. Because, and I cannot stress this enough, when I referred Jose and his girlfriend for a criminality check, "routine" was the operative word.

One of the main jobs of the CBSA is to determine the admissibility of foreign nationals seeking entry to Canada. Canadians, Permanent Residents, and Status Indians may enter by right. Everyone else is granted entry at our discretion. That entry often involves a risk assessment. Part of that risk assessment may be a check of the traveler's criminal history.

By reciprocal arrangement with the US, Canadian peace officers may access the NCIC computer system, which stores police records from all across the USA. We routinely access this in our work, but this requires us to conduct a more in-depth examination inside the office. Many inadmissible people are admitted because the officer does not know that they are inadmissible.

A certain amount of instinct is required. Jose and his girlfriend were coming up to Vancouver for the weekend. They'd never been to Canada before; so, they'd never been checked. Plus, Jose, a clean-cut looking young man with no obvious red flags about his appearance, kept looking down that road.

I know that look. It says, *I need to get past you.* It invites attention. I handed Jose his referral card, and his face dropped. That says, *this is not going according to plan.*

It's a dangerous moment. People do run the border, and we depend on the RCMP to catch them. They sometimes do. Because they're running, they put everyone else on the road at risk. You must carefully monitor your nervous driver, and communicate with the point officer, to make sure he gets inside.

Jose did what he was told, and he and his girlfriend went inside. I've always wondered since; did he realize what was in his phone? Why didn't he delete it? Why didn't he hide it in the car? Drop it down a storm drain?

The answer is probably quite prosaic: He probably had no idea that anyone would try and look in his phone. So, he walked into the office with it on his person.

I was relieved from the road, and found them standing inside the office, so I called them up, performed a perfunctory pocket check for weapons, and took their phones. Jose leaned nonchalantly on the counter.

"I'm going to have a look in your phone. Is there anything in there that you're concerned about me seeing?"

"No."

"Is your phone locked?"

"Nope."

Honestly, I had no idea what was coming. *He was so cool. And his phone wasn't even locked!*

The first hint of trouble for Jose, who had no criminal record, were the messages about drugs. At first, it seemed like he was a small-time pot dealer. Yawn. But then, the talk about drugs spread to other, harder stuff. And it began to sound as if Jose was driving far and wide, not just to sell drugs, but to organize importation and distribution.

People like Jose are the golden 1% all border officers are waiting to meet. I figured I might have a serious dope seizure on my hands. But then, I came across a text exchange with a man named Jesus.

Jesus was very worried. He was very worried that someone might have seen he and Jose a couple of weeks before in Seattle.

The reason he was worried was because, at that time, he and Jose were chasing the occupants of a BMW through the streets, trying to kill them with an AK-47 and a Glock pistol. Helpfully, they even included media links.

From this, I realized that I had a murderer on my hands. The driver of the BMW, who apparently had some minor tiff with Jose and Jesus in a nightclub, was dead. His front seat passenger was seriously injured. The two girls in the back seat were unharmed.

The police, the media stories said, had no leads.

I held the phone in my trembling hand. I called Jessie to come and meet me in the intelligence office. He arrived with Sheldon. I told them what I had.

"Holy shit." They said in unison. We talked strategy, and decided the best course of action, since the crime had occurred outside of Canada, was to detain Jose for a hearing under Immigration law. There is a clause which allows officers to detain, and then direct a foreign national suspected of having committed a serious crime, back to the US pending a future hearing.

This would allow us to get our gunman, and his phone, into the hands of US Customs. But how to conduct the interview which Immigration law called for? I knew my limitations: I was not a homicide dick, and there was no way I was going to conduct a homicide interrogation lest I fuck it up completely.

Luckily, the evidence of narcotics trafficking also constituted serious criminal activity for our purposes. We could simply choose to focus on that.

Let me tell you, this was never covered in Rigaud. We were making it up as we went along. Luckily, I had good officers backing me up, and a Superintendent who wasn't afraid to make a decision. "Let's do it," Jessie agreed, "But how do we take him in?"

By this time, Terry, now a force instructor, had joined the discussion. "Code Five. He's a murder suspect."

I demurred, perhaps too cautious now. "I don't know. I did a pocket check."

Sheldon wasn't buying it. "So, you're sure he doesn't have a gun?"

I chewed a nail. "Pretty sure."

"Not good enough." Sheldon shook his head. "If I'm going in there with you, we're following our training. We're doing it at gunpoint."

He was right. "Fine. Let's call him out and take him outside."

Luckily, it was a quiet night. We set up outside, then called Jose out. He walked out, somewhat nervous, then downright shocked when I drew down and had him prone out.

The girlfriend went ballistic, apparently ignorant of the fact that Jose was a stone-cold killer. Sheldon, who had an ability to charm women I've only seen in movies, was able to get her calmed down.

But Jose was not calming down. By the time Jessie and I got him into an interview room, he was giving us that back and forth, swiveling headed, *what have you got on me* look. I was nervous. I'd chartered and cautioned him, even though, technically in an Immigration case the caution against statements did not apply.

But I was thinking down the road, to a murder trial. Would a US court introduce into evidence what they would view as a compelled statement? Not a goddamned chance. Luckily, he waived counsel. What would a lawyer have made of this?

When I explained to him why he was here, the reaction was telling. "Messages? What kind of messages?"

He didn't seem to object much when I told him he was a drug trafficker, drug traffickers weren't welcome in Canada, and he was going back to the States. That told me all I needed to know. He was probably happy we weren't grilling him for a death penalty offence.

One slip, and we could've had a refugee claim on our hands, and a much more complicated situation. But we kept it short, and sweet. Within the hour, we had him back in the USA, with the evidence safely in the hands of an ICE agent.

The day after, I was on a plane headed for Brazil. When I came back a month later, I was asked to write a brief for the King County DA on Canadian border search law. I figured that was more a case for the Justice Department, but I relished the challenge, so I prepared a seven-page brief.

It turned out that, somewhere along the way, the ball had been dropped. Somehow, both men were now fugitives from justice. Jose had been released, then actually returned to Seattle PD for an interview. For whatever reason, they didn't lock him up then, but when they called him back again, he'd split.

Both men were believed to have fled to Mexico. In the text messages, Jesus had already been talking about going to California. I felt bad for the victims, and their families, but what could I do? We'd all done what we could, but it wasn't really our case.

Years went by with no word. Then, the summer before I retired, I was congratulated by the Chief as I entered the office. "Okay? What did I do?"

"They caught one of your guys. He's being extradited from California."

Seems that Jesus was missing water you could drink, so he turned himself in. But I never heard any more about the case, or what happened to Jose. So, I solved a murder, but was justice ever served?

And would I have searched that phone a few years later? The answer is no.

If you're such a fan of privacy that you're okay with that, then hats off.

At least, you have the courage of your convictions. Just don't piss off Jose in a bar and expect to live.

FIFTY-ONE

THE BIG LIE

As I drifted towards pre-retirement apathy in the last few years of my career, I began pensively checking my retirement calculator. This handy little application would tell a member of the Public Service just how far he had to go, based on years of service, rank, highest pay grade, etc.

I hadn't yet entirely made up my mind to quit; but I was drifting closer every day.

My dad had always counselled me to make up a "pros and cons" list prior to making any big decision. I knew this would be as big a decision as parenthood, and just as irreversible: Once I left, I knew there was no way in hell they'd ever take me back. I'd said too much, tilted too many windmills, argued with too many people who weren't used to being challenged.

When I first started compiling these pro/con lists, back in 2011 during a rough year for me, the cons far outweighed the pros. They continued to, well into 2015.

But three factors now tipped the scale for me: One was the election of Justin Trudeau. Having worked for the Liberals before, I knew that national security concerns of any kind were alien territory to them. They simply did not care. The second factor was the general wave of anti-police sentiment arising in North America since 2014. It had always been a difficult job. Now, it showed signs of becoming an impossible one.

I am no martyr. I am a man who was quite comfortable putting "husband and father" over "peace officer" on my self-identification template. I have no desire to lay down my life for people who want to send me to prison.

But the third, and probably deciding factor was that I now realized unequivocally that I was working for liars. Big, pants-on-fire liars whose whoppers could make Goebbels blush.

People are who they associate with, and to a certain extent, who they serve. Many cops have a certain perverse pride in swimming upstream; that is, trying to be a moral actor in an amoral organization. The gradual shift away from rock-solid, military-grade ideals towards slimy corporatism in law enforcement culture has been the work of decades. But I believed that we had reached something of an Omega Point in our moral inversion. The best people's only chance of getting promoted was through sheer accident, or, in the case of certain pesky union types, through being brought into the tent to piss out.

The Agency had brought in po-faced integrity lecturers to whip our supposedly corrupt asses into shape after all of our traitor-related scandals. Nobody mentioned how popular all of the traitors were with management, or the numerous ethical lapses on the part of our supposed betters; no, this was somehow all our fault.

Discipline got mean, management got petty, and people like me doubled the size of the chips on their shoulders overnight.

You see, the big problem with "integrity" was that I could, if given the time, point squarely at a singular instance in which the CBSA had been lying to the public for decades. They'd even been lying, at least through omission, to their law enforcement partners.

This big lie was all about CPIC on the front line. Allow me to explain.

CPIC, or the Canadian Police Information Centre, is the national repository of criminal intelligence and charges and convictions. CBSA has access to CPIC, but there's a catch.

Before I talk, obliquely of course, about what this catch is, let me tell you what the big lie was, and how the world finally found out part of it. Because I swore a secrecy oath, I cannot disclose certain things, even if I am damned certain those things are in the public interest to know.

The big lie is this: The CBSA views protecting the public as its top priority. As part of this sacred duty, it uses "smart" information technology to risk-assess travellers prior to their entry into Canada.

This is a monumental lie. CBSA's top priority is actually twofold: To minimize both border wait times and complaints. This is why the officer *in the booth* has less information at his fingertips than a Special Constable in Toronto.

If an officer decides, largely on a hunch, to refer someone for an examination, then the full capabilities of CPIC can be brought to bear. But only then.

This tap-dancing around the truth goes back a long way. As a shop steward representing union members facing discipline, I spent a lot of time researching Labour Relations tribunal decisions. One interesting one I came across was from Coutts, Alberta, wherein the locals had decided they were sick of being in the dark out there and decided to grieve the *Armed and Dangerous* lookout process.

In the absence of a proper interface with CPIC, officers depended on the Intelligence Division to give them timely and actionable information on deadly threats. A police officer on the road has this information as a matter of course; but CBSA officers stand two steps removed from it. First, someone has to be aware of this information, and decide to put it into a CBSA database. Second, they have to be authorized to do so.

There are a number of hurdles at work here. First, already overworked Intelligence officers must actively seek out high-risk suspects, usually through media reports, and gather the information on them all on their own. In later years, I took this job on myself, to the consternation of my superiors. But I always had Chris in my corner, and nobody was ever ready to tell me "no." I suppose they guessed what my reply would be.

Once you've got the information, you've got to get it authorized. There's the big hurdle. The biggest hurdle of all was *Armed and Dangerous* cautions.

Generally speaking, CBSA officers were not fired up to go catch bicycle thieves. We were worried about the same people who keep you up at night. But there was a whole layer of officialdom more concerned with keeping officers' guns in holsters. Because our training to take down armed and dangerous suspects was the "high-risk-takedown," i.e., draw gun, take cover, issue commands, there was an insidious pressure to limit the number of high-risk takedowns made.

That pressure led to some truly egregious safety gambles. In Quebec, an Intelligence Officer classified a suspect in a triple homicide as an auto theft suspect, not even bothering to issue a caution. After protest at the more bold-faced minimizations and deceptions of the Intelligence Division began to build, a new risk category called "Known to Carry Weapons" emerged. This allowed CBSA to seem that it had warned its staff, while at the same time restricting officers' use of proper tactical responses.

I told my bosses then: If I see "Known to Carry Weapons," I draw. I've got a big file full of cases to justify that decision, like so:

RCMP: Armed and Dangerous
CBSA: Known to Carry Weapons
QED: Draw, and grab some cover, son.

The people at Coutts called the CBSA on this sort of bullshit. This case wound up in front of Labour Relations, and as it pre-dated the arming of officers, it highlights the other reason for CBSA suppressing this information.

Under Canadian Labour Law, any employee may refuse unsafe work. Unarmed CBSA officers processing armed suspects would certainly count, so CBSA would clearly be tempted to limit information on cases which might prompt a work refusal.

When the case went to tribunal, CBSA boldly argued that there was no way CPIC could be hooked up to primary line booths. The delays would simply be too great. Rather than call up the local RCMP detachment for a second opinion, the tribunal bought it, hook, line, and sinker. The grievance was denied.

But the bold actions of the Coutts officers would bear fruit years later. They couldn't have imagined how.

A few years before retirement, a story on the CBC website caught my eye. A rape victim in London, Ontario was astonished to see her rapist in the newsletter of her local church.

She was astonished because, years before, she'd filed a full police complaint at the time of her assault, which had been diligently investigated by the local police. The police had issued a warrant for the man, who'd unfortunately fled the country.

The man was a Nigerian priest. Nigerians require visas to visit Canada. He got another visa, despite having an active, Canada-wide arrest warrant for a serious offence, and he presented his legal identification at a CBSA crossing. He was admitted. Again, he got out before the victim got justice.

The London Police did not understand how this could have happened. Neither did the CBC, whose attempts to get the CBSA to explain this apparent gross security lapse were met with standard-issue boilerplate reassurance.

Reading the story, I felt my blood boiling in my ears. It was one thing for CBSA to willfully risk the lives of armed officers by withholding information; quite another thing to victimize a woman twice for the sake of satisfying their own twisted prerogatives.

I had to do something, but what? I am no Edward Snowden. Secrecy means something to me, even when I feel it is being abused. What gives me the right to make a unilateral decision to abrogate my oath?

But then I remembered the Labour Relations case in Coutts. *That* was a matter of public record, requiring no disclosure of classified information. When I got home, I looked up the CBC reporter's e-mail, and sent him a link. "I can't tell you, but…"

Within a week, the CBSA had been forced to admit a glaring hole in Canada's security. All of a sudden, that which could not be fixed, was, suddenly, fixed. In a freaking week.

I never thought I'd go all "Deep Throat." But when disclosure is the only way to right a glaring wrong; when there is no other way to protect the innocent, what do you do? I know the Rigaud answer. I also knew it was wrong.

Apropos of nothing: I read, just before I wrote this chapter, of a police pursuit in Ontario in which a man wanted for murder in Houston, Texas was killed. Apparently, the CBSA was still looking into how he'd gotten into Canada.

My, my, I wonder. Though the Nigerian priest case solved part of our glaring security problem, other problems remain. Get my drift? I sure hope somebody does…

FIFTY-TWO

ARMED CLERKS

Oh, where to begin with all the adventures of the last couple of years of my career?

Um, well, to be honest, I don't remember much. Most of the interesting things I've already talked about. In the last year before I retired, my arrests dipped into the single digits, probably for the first time in my career.

Why did this happen? It was a combination of factors. The largest single one being, Immigration permit work had now, well and truly, become the number one priority of POE Douglas. Like I've said before, we were spending 75% of our available time doing things which bored and frustrated us. That which we were good at could only be done if time permitted. In 2019, with some 6500 frontline staff, the agency only managed to seize 675 firearms. That's just over one for every 10 officers, roughly. If you take away officers in modes unlikely to encounter many guns, such as Air Traffic, the ratio is closer to 1:20. When I first came to the border, it was not unusual to encounter officers whose numbers, individually, were in the double digits.

Clearly, something had been lost. Emphasis on Immigration processing meant there was little time to search. Emphasis on wait times meant what was searched was often rushed.

And reliance on the computer to make decisions meant good, selective referrals based on knowledge and experience were rarer and rarer. At the same time, officers could face draconian discipline for missing a lookout generated by the computer, even if the information was inaccurate or did not exactly match.

This terrified newer staff into sticking to what was safe. Obey the computer. Don't miss anything. Rely on targeting. Targeting will tell us what to do.

We gutted our intelligence division in 2011 as part of a clumsy move to recoup budget deficits arising from the Great Recession of 2008. Therefore, we relied on targeters instead.

Targeters were cheaper because they didn't need the full training and equipment of a peace officer. They were generally hired right out of university, and sent to HQ, where they applied algorithms to tell us what to do. Their knowledge of the border was strictly theoretical.

I once had this conversation with a targeter:

"You've flagged this guy for his travel, right?"

"Yes. Very suspicious. He's crossing into Canada ten times a week. Always at two ports."

"Are those two ports Boundary Bay and Douglas?"

"Wait...how did you know that?"

"And is he crossing into Boundary Bay in the morning, and Douglas in the afternoon?"

"Well...yes. Yes he is. How did you..."

"He's a commuter. He lives in Point Roberts and works in Bellingham. Take another look at the map." I hung up the phone and released the guy.

But the agency persisted in its stubborn belief that local knowledge could not compete with the wisdom of Ottawa. In the meantime, intelligence lost credibility worth the rank-and-file.

We were told nothing, so we got nothing. We went without a detector dog for months. We lost scores of officers to the expanding Transit Police, then to the Mounties, then to VPD.

A year after I retired, I ran into a friend of mine who was a Superintendent at Douglas. "What's your authorized strength?"

"100."

"How many have you actually got?"

"50."

Stripped to the bones, the operation ran on fumes. As long as the wait times were kept under one hour, and the permits got processed, nobody seemed to care. Everyone around me who was smart enough to notice the problems, or with enough integrity to care about them, had the same hangdog look I recognized from my own face in the mirror.

The bosses did not care. In 2014, they flexed their muscles, and showed that muscle was what they had between their ears, when they dropped the hammer on a supervisor and his staff in Emerson, Manitoba.

Their crime? Sending a detachment, not all the staff, but a small detachment, to back up outnumbered Mounties executing a high-risk kidnapping warrant in a nearby hotel. The Mounties had asked for their help, the nearest RCMP backup being 45 minutes away, and perhaps the bosses were not cognizant of this fact but refusing such a request without lawful excuse was actually illegal.

The average citizen might be able to avoid conviction, but armed and trained peace officers did not have such a good excuse. The port was not left unattended, and the situation was resolved peacefully. The RCMP were appreciative.

The Director wanted blood, and Portelance was happy to help. All the officers received lengthy suspensions. The case aroused media and public interest, with the pointed question, "Why are cops getting in trouble for helping other cops protect the public?" being put pointedly.

But the CBSA did not want their staff to see themselves as cops. And they smelled an incoming Liberal government on the wind. So, when the outgoing Minister of Public Safety demanded an explanation for the suspensions, he got...silence.

In October 2015, the Liberal government returned in an overwhelming majority victory. Justin Trudeau returned the CBSA managers to their comfort zone. I knew things could only get worse.

The election of Trudeau convinced me, along with some other factors I've already mentioned, that it was time to leave. Informally, I told my wife that 2016, the year of the publication of my first novel, would also be my last full year as a CBSA officer.

In the meantime, I stamped this form, and that. I did it on autopilot. If Canada didn't care, why should I?

I'd retired already. They'd just forgotten to take the gun and the badge.

FIFTY-THREE

GOODBYEEE

In the final episode of *Blackadder Goes Forth*, Captain Blackadder and his motley crew go over the top into the German machine guns, an exercise in complete futility, but absolute nobility.

I was not asked to submit myself to pointless mass slaughter. But as my career drew to an end, I began to feel the futility. What had we been doing? What was the point of busting our asses to intercept dope, when it was being handed out for nothing in the worst hit areas?

What was the point of busting our asses to seize guns, when the government's response was to eliminate mandatory minimum sentences for gun crimes, opting to demonize legal gun owners instead?

And why bother taking the risks of always leading, always speaking out, when you knew that you were despised, and would never receive the slightest reward?

If this sounds like a bit of a pity party, it probably is. But there was truth in it, too. I'd grown sick of doing what was right with the knowledge of its having been right supposed to be my reward. I'd watched others be rewarded and celebrated for far less.

But I'd also seen people who'd done, or suffered, far more than me, be treated even worse.

I guess I just got tired of having to bring the same shit up, again and again, without result. I felt like Bill Murray in *Groundhog Day,* hitting the snooze button, over and over.

In the end, it wasn't about recognition, or hurt feelings, or money. It was about life.

I had two daughters now. This had rearranged my priorities, as it does for many new parents. But I had thoughts many of those new parents did not have to contend with. The Pac Highway Five incident had convinced me that the agency did not stand behind its own training. I might very well be forced to choose between my job or my life, but if I survived a deadly encounter, how would I provide for my kids? If an over-zealous prosecutor decided to make me a trophy skull, how would I explain to my kids that daddy was going to prison?

Lori's shooting, and the flaccid, dishonest response of the CBSA afterward, convinced me that a cost/benefit analysis in Ottawa had determined the following: I was expendable. As was Lori, as were the rest of us Bozos. This was an agency that cared so little about us that they fucked and farted around while their useless Phoenix pay system put people out of their homes.

I never particularly minded risking my life to protect my community, and my country. But, as a rising tide of anti-police sentiment swept North America, I began to wonder why I was bothering.

Besides, I'd found something I liked better than law enforcement: writing. I'd released my first novel in 2016, and my second was due to come in 2017. I wasn't making a cent on it. But I was determined to keep trying until I broke through. And I was determined to make a future where I was in charge.

Part of the price of carrying a badge and a gun is being treated like a child. I'd grown tired of sitting outside the Chief's office like a bad little boy waiting for the principal. Fuck the principal. I was approaching middle age, and I was the one who wanted to be called "sir." The power of a badge and a gun was nothing but an illusion. I knew that now. I wanted to be my own boss, even if it meant living with less. I wanted to spend more time with my family, even if it meant being able to give them less.

Plus, I'd done everything I'd wanted to do on the job. I'd caught every kind of case imaginable, more than I could have ever imagined when I first started. The only thing I hadn't encountered, was the one thing I didn't want to find out about: A deadly force incident. I was happy to leave that one uncertain.

A few months before I left, I encountered the most massive asshole I'd ever met on the job. And by that, I mean, he was an asshole, and he was physically massive. 6'8, 350 pounds, biceps the size of softballs, bulging veins, and simmering menace.

I looked around the office. Empty. I was Eastwood, he was Van Cleef. There were no tumbleweeds, but it would have been appropriate. I got on the radio.

"That's right." He smirked. "You're gonna need backup."

I felt for my baton, resigned to breaking some bones. "Okay. But either way, you're gonna lose."

Finally, my backup showed, and I got him to play along. But what really bothered me was the technicolour dream I had afterward. I imagined fucking that big bastard up every way I could. The blood ran, the teeth flew.

I woke up, sickened. I was tired of a lot of things, but I was also tired of violence. Dealing it, being subjected to it, dealing with its aftermath, even preparing every day for its potential use.

When I put in my letter of resignation, I felt suddenly lighter. I'd miss the people. I'd never miss the bullshit.

I think I'm a calmer person now, more...normal. Sometimes, I find it hard to believe that I ever did this job. Then, I remember.

I make do with less, materially. But I have more time with people who matter to me. And I no longer worry about being destitute suddenly, or going to prison, for doing my job. I no longer have to visualize my wife getting that folded flag.

If you want to serve, serve. I spent the first half of my life dreaming of serving. Eventually, I did, and regardless of what I've said, I don't regret it. But when the time came to leave, I did so, without regard for the pension clock, the golden promise of something more, that you may or may not live to receive.

Whatever you do, check out on your own terms. Serve, do your duty, gather your stories, and leave when you want to.

I did. And I don't regret it.

EPILOGUE: OF FENCES AND FREEDOM

I'm writing this epilogue in the second month of a pandemic lockdown. A lockdown really only made possible by the existence of borders.

I'm not on the frontline anymore. I've been out three years, and honestly it feels like three centuries.

As the old cop saying goes, "When you're in, you're the best. When you're out, you're a pest."

It's true, really. My kids wonder why I don't go down to the border anymore. They wouldn't understand if I told them; I am yesterday's news.

This is not self-pity; it's simply reality. Law Enforcement is a forward-looking culture. It's no country for old men. I've written lots of stories as a writer, but as a cop? I've written all the stories I will ever write. I have no more to give, and that's okay.

In my last three years, in particular, I began to feel that my tank was running on empty. Like I couldn't give 100% if I had to. And that mattered to me. I always wanted to give 100%. When I couldn't anymore, it was time to exit stage left.

To every law enforcement officer considering retirement: let me say this: Have a second act. You need to have a second act. My father never did. He figured that he could rest on the laurels on 31 years of service to his country. He was certainly justified in moral terms.

But a brain at rest is no more fit than a bicep at rest. It grows flaccid and flabby. The only thing that keeps me sane today is my life as a writer. If it weren't for that, I'd be doing nothing more than recounting war stories to slobbery drunks at a bar.

Come to think of it, I simply do a more a literate version of this. But hey, "writer" sounds better than "barfly." Ask Bukowski.

What can I give? I can talk about my experiences. I can speak, with the freedom denied to those still serving. I can counsel without fear of the bullies at the top of the pyramid; of the complaint mongering lawyers and activists; of the rabble-rousing reporters.

To all of you, I say sincerely: fuck you all. You contribute precious little to the society you claim to protect. Not 10% of that contributed by the men and women whom you claim to hold in check. Eat a bag of dicks. Mustard's on me.

So, back to the point of the whole exercise. Back to borders.

Borders have not been very popular of late. An entire political conglomeration, the European Union, has been sold largely on its abolition of border controls; six months ago, the leading talking point among Democratic Presidential candidates in the United States was an open border.

And now? Where do we stand now? Plastic bags, disposable straws, and border controls are now back in fashion. The idea that borders might protect us, rather than simply slow us down for no reason, is gaining currency.

It is no great stretch to suggest that, if Canada had followed the example of Taiwan, and implemented strict border controls on travel from China, that we could've avoided our current reality of no restaurants, no schools, and no vacations. We could have been freer. But now, we are prisoners in our own homes, while the residents of Taipei can go shopping.

Can fences bring freedom? What a curious, seemingly contradictory idea. Granted, we don't live in an era of deep thinking, but this one merits consideration: what if a few limits on our freedoms, a few intrusions by the state, could result in greater freedom in the long run?

Consider the case of a neighbourhood suffering under a reign of gang terror. They have to dive under their furniture, and run from cover in the playground, because of the actions of people who live next door to them. These people have guns, not legally obtained, of course, and not interdicted at the border, where they have been smuggled in from the United States.

There are people, supposedly quite concerned with the rights of the people who live in this neighbourhood. But they are entirely focused on the people who deal with the violence, not the ones who deal it out. In their view, the police officer who stops and questions the young man of colour, the one with the dubious bulge in his waistband; he is the one who merits watching. In the view of the rights industry, the border officer who demands a password for a cell phone in the possession of a suspected gun smuggler; he is the problem, not the smuggler.

But it is not the police and the border officers who make the children dive for cover in a place where they should feel safe; this is the work of the ones the rights industry protects. The people they strive to free, early and often, so they may return to their devil's work.

What I am suggesting is that borders may be good for liberty. Nosy cops who prevent shootings, rather than merely respond to them, may be the guardians of liberty. Fences may mean freedom.

Yesterday, the Liberal government announced a blanket ban on what they like to call "assault weapons." In reality, all such weapons that would be used by a military as "assault weapons" have been illegal for decades. What the government is doing is targeting weapons that look scary. The obedient and helpful media slavishly point out that some of these guns have been used in mass shootings. Yes, they have been. But the list of weapons to be banned extends to 1500 weapons.

Of course, there's money for enforcement at the border too. 87 million dollars!

As a former officer, I can almost certainly guarantee that this money will be diverted to furniture, travel, executive bonuses, and "fact-finding." Precious little of the very little allocated will be spent on frontline resources. I predict a few x-ray trailers, sitting around gathering dust.

If fences mean freedom, our fences need work. We have a large agency supposedly dedicated to border security, but it woefully underperforms when it comes to seizing the American guns used in most Canadian gun crime.

Why can't the CBSA do things right? Is there any hope, or is it time to start over?

As a fish rots from the head, so too does the CBSA. The problem begins in the executive suite. Almost none of the executives at the national level have ever served in any law enforcement capacity. Most of their subordinates in Headquarters never have, either.

This is a situation unique in a major law enforcement agency. It's like hiring a bunch of aerospace engineers to run a bakery. The bagels might come out very aerodynamic, but perhaps not taste as good with cream cheese and lox.

This curious situation results in some obvious problems. One is a central distaste and fear of the natural mission people expect of the CBSA. Policing can be an ugly business. There are guns, people get hurt, they complain. Executives straight from Heritage Canada can have a hard time dealing with this.

Another problem is role confusion. Given mandated roles in the administration of more than 70 pieces of federal legislation, the hapless mandarins cannot decide which ones should be priorities.

The CBSA has a hard time saying "No." I recall many years of us doing boat registrations for Transport Canada, before somebody finally wondered aloud why this was our job in the first place. Today, the big problem is the downloading of Citizenship and Immigration paperwork to the POEs, which is crippling their ability to free up staff to interdict contraband.

This role confusion leads to confusion about who should be hired. There is no possibility that the agency can find a person as interested in exotic animals as they are in seizing guns and drugs. This results in some very round pegs in some very square holes.

Other problems share more in common with other law enforcement agencies. A culture of risk-aversion which leads to the promotion of grey people, uninspiring, risk-averse leaders. A culture of secrecy, which puts the agency always behind the eight-ball, never able to catch up with the pace of social media.

This risk-averse culture results in managers only too glad to hand over what should be their work to the RCMP.

Morley Lymburner, the former editor of Blue Line Magazine, and a former Toronto street cop, once referred to the CBSA as "tragically underutilized." I think what he meant was, the CBSA has a large number of very capable people, the vagaries of recruiting notwithstanding, who could, if utilized properly, provide Canada with the border security she desperately needs.

The moment is now; there can be no delay. The public lacks confidence in the immigration and refugee systems. The Roxham Road debacle, with lineups of suitcase-toting economic migrants posing as refugees and using RCMP officers as porters, does not help. While being asked to abandon their property for the sake of a safer Canada, people must accept the reality of a CBSA that literally cannot find its own ass in an outhouse. We fail to interdict wanted criminals, terrorists, and smugglers. Most of the problems are easily fixable.

They simply require two solutions: First, Common sense; Second: Honesty. Identify the problem, then please, stop lying about it.

What would I do, if I became President of the CBSA tomorrow?

First, I would purge the executive ranks, bringing in experienced law enforcement professionals to take their places. Then, these professionals would have to make some decisions.

Who, and how to hire, is the most crucial. As we saw in the chapter "Traitors," corruption and lack of integrity has crippled the CBSA. Rather than treat all officers as under suspicion, perhaps we ought to bring in proper background checks and stress interviews for new hires, and subject those seeking an increase in security clearance to proper procedure, similar to that employed by our law enforcement partners.

We cannot staff the frontiers with people we cannot trust. The issue of integrity must be addressed, immediately. I am confident, from my experience, that only perhaps 3 in every 100 people will be a problem. But those problems must be rooted out.

Once hired, recruits must be given training that prepares them for the reality of modern border policing. Who gives a shit where people's clothes were made? What does heroin look like, how do you safe an AK-47, what symbols does a Nazi wear, how do pedophiles conceal their filth; these are far more important. This training must continue in the field, with proper guidance and correction from senior officers, supported by management.

Improved leadership is not possible without a Senior Officer rank to support and assist the Superintendents. Too much is now asked of the Superintendents, and too little of the senior staff, who, in many cases, are ready and willing to take on more. A new rank, not supervisory, and still in the union, but recognized as having a field leadership role, would only be acknowledging the truth that Jim, Graydon, Terry, myself, and so many other senior staff lived.

Border officers confront the reality of the most heavily armed civil society in the world, the United States of America. They must be equipped properly to face this challenge. There is no reason at all why the average CBSA officer should not have access to Taser, shotguns, and patrol carbines while on duty. Having seized enough semi-automatic, and sometimes fully automatic weapons, I can testify this is an absolute necessity. All of the lessons of the bloodbaths of the last fifteen years in Canadian law enforcement must be applied to the CBSA. When seconds count, we cannot wait for minutes. Mayerthorpe and Moncton, and now, Portapique, are lessons which must be applied to us. That Andrew Crews stopped when he did and had only a handgun instead of something far worse; these were blessings, not certainties. We cannot count on them again.

When people run our border, we must be trained and equipped to give chase immediately. We cannot know why they are running, but we can certainly suspect, based on past experience, that the reason is malicious. All CBSA officers must be properly trained in pursuit driving and indemnified for same.

We must revitalize our Intelligence and Investigations Divisions, in order to support our front line as effectively as possible.

We must end the practice of using POEs as permit mills. Let Citizenship and Immigration clerks perform the work of clerks; there is no good reason to pay officers 80,000 CAD a year to do this work.

With more manpower to take on the problems of the border, we must act to address the critical weaknesses of our frontier. We must renegotiate the ridiculous "Safe-Third-Country" agreement to short-circuit fraudulent refugee claims. And we must place border enforcement solely in the hands of the agency uniquely equipped to deal with it: the CBSA.

The CBSA can, will, and should perform almost all border law enforcement functions. Operating as part of an integrated team with local law enforcement, sharing frequencies, and resources such as helicopters and K-9 teams, a mature border service would finally emerge from the shadows to take its place as an equal.

Border policing IS policing. It's that simple. I held on for years, hoping the agency would acknowledge that self-evident fact, to no avail.

 Now, I can say what I want. Maybe I can do more good outside, than in.

The change still needs to happen. Take a good look and see if you agree. The portcullis is broken. Let us fix it, together.

OTHER BOOKS BY THE AUTHOR

Fiction:

The Will Bryant Thrillers:

Southern Cross

Back in Slowly

The Wolf of Penha

Only the Dead

Spectrum

Other Fiction:

Goodtime Charlie

When Yer Number's Up

Bomber's Moon

Slowly, The World Burns, While I Help to Fan the Flames

The Troika of Osip Teitelbaum

Non-Fiction:

Acts and Offences: Opinion, 2017-2020

A Life on the Line

All available from Amazon as print and e-books.

Made in the USA
Monee, IL
12 March 2021